# C++ Programming for Beginners

I0408619

*The Comprehensive Guide*

MAXWELL RIVERS

# INTRODUCTION

Welcome to "C++ Programming for Beginners." Whether you're a complete novice in the world of programming or you have some experience with other languages, this book is your gateway to mastering the art of C++ programming.

## Why Learn C++?

C++ is a powerful and versatile programming language that has stood the test of time. Developed in the early 1980s by Bjarne Stroustrup, C++ has since become one of the most widely used programming languages in the world. It's the language behind many of the software applications, games, operating systems, and even embedded systems that we use daily.

So, why should you learn C++ in this era of numerous programming languages? Here are a few compelling reasons:

1. Industry Demand:

C++ remains in high demand in the job market, especially for roles in software development, game development, and systems programming. By learning C++, you open doors to exciting and lucrative career opportunities.

2. Performance:

C++ is known for its exceptional performance. It allows you to write code that runs efficiently and has low-level control over hardware, making it an ideal choice for resource-intensive applications.

3. Versatility:

C++ is a multi-paradigm language, which means you can use it for a wide range of programming tasks, from low-level system programming to high-level application development. It offers both procedural and object-oriented programming capabilities.

4. Foundation for Learning:

Learning C++ provides a solid foundation for understanding other programming languages. Once you grasp the concepts and principles of C++, transitioning to other languages becomes much smoother.

# What You'll Find in This Book

This book is designed with beginners in mind. Whether you're a student, a hobbyist, or someone looking to kickstart a career in programming, you'll find the content here accessible and informative. We'll start from the very basics and gradually build your knowledge and skills.

Here's a glimpse of what you can expect to learn in the chapters ahead:

- **Getting Started with C++:** We'll introduce you to the fundamentals of C++, setting up your development environment, and writing your first program.
- **Variables and Data Types:** You'll understand how to work with data in C++, including different data types, variables, constants, and type conversions.
- **Control Flow:** We'll cover the essential concepts of making decisions and looping in your programs.
- **Functions:** You'll learn how to write reusable code using functions and understand the principles of scope and recursion.
- **Object-Oriented Programming:** Discover the power of C++'s object-oriented features, including classes, inheritance, polymorphism, and more.
- **Exception Handling:** Learn to handle errors and exceptions gracefully in your programs.
- **File Handling:** Explore how to read from and write to files, an essential skill for many real-world applications.

- **STL (Standard Template Library):** Dive into the rich set of data structures and algorithms provided by the STL, which can save you time and effort in your coding projects.
- **Best Practices and Coding Style:** We'll emphasize good coding practices and help you write clean, maintainable, and efficient code.
- **Final Projects and Real-World Applications:** Apply your newfound knowledge to create practical projects and gain insight into how C++ is used in various industries.

## How to Use This Book

This book is structured to be both a comprehensive reference and a hands-on guide. Each chapter builds upon the knowledge gained from the previous one. We encourage you to follow along with the examples, practice the exercises, and, most importantly, write your code. The more you code, the more proficient you'll become.

Remember, learning to program is a journey, and it's okay to make mistakes along the way. In fact, making mistakes and learning from them is an essential part of the process. Embrace challenges, ask questions, and explore beyond the book's content.

By the time you reach the end of this book, you'll have a solid understanding of C++ and the confidence to tackle your programming projects.

Happy coding!

# CONTENTS

# 1: GETTING STARTED WITH C++

## 1.1 Understanding the Basics

Before we dive into writing your first C++ program, it's essential to grasp some fundamental concepts about programming, the role of a programming language, and how computers interpret and execute code.

**What is Programming?**

Programming is the process of instructing a computer to perform a specific task or a series of tasks. At its core, a computer is a powerful but dumb machine that can execute instructions at an incredible speed. These instructions, or lines of code, are what programmers write to tell the computer what to do.

*The Role of a Programming Language*

To communicate with a computer, we use programming languages like C++. Think of a programming language as a bridge between human-readable instructions and machine-executable actions.

C++ is known as a high-level programming language because it's closer to human language, making it relatively easy for us to understand and write. However, computers don't understand C++ directly. They require a translation step, performed by a **compiler**, to convert our C++ code into a language called **machine code** that the computer can execute.

## How Code is Executed

When you write a C++ program, it consists of a series of statements that are executed one after the other. This sequential execution is the fundamental behavior of most computer programs. Let's break down this process:

1. **Writing Code:** You write C++ code in a text editor or integrated development environment (IDE). This code is a set of instructions to be executed.
2. **Compiling Code:** After writing your code, you run it through a C++ **compiler**, which checks for errors and translates your human-readable code into machine code. The output is a binary file or an executable program.
3. **Running the Program:** You execute the compiled program. The computer loads it into memory and starts executing the instructions one by one.
4. **Output and Actions:** As the program runs, it can produce output, perform calculations, interact with the user, or manipulate data. The computer follows the instructions precisely, step by step.
5. **Termination:** The program continues to execute until it reaches the end, or until you instruct it to stop. At this point, it might produce final output or perform cleanup operations.

## The Power of Programming

Programming allows us to automate tasks, process data, solve complex problems, and create software applications that range from simple utilities to advanced video games and intricate scientific simulations. It's a skill that empowers you to turn your ideas into digital reality and to contribute to countless fields, from business and science to art and entertainment.

# 1.2 Your First C++ Program

Congratulations on taking your first steps into the world of C++ programming! In this section, we'll guide you through the process of writing and running your very first C++ program. Don't worry if you're new to programming—by the end of this section, you'll have a solid understanding of how to create and execute a basic C++ program.

**The Anatomy of a C++ Program**

Before we write our first program, let's take a quick look at the essential components that make up a C++ program:

```
#include <iostream>

int main() {
    // Your code goes here

    return 0;
}
```

Let's break this down:

- #include <iostream>: This line includes a library called iostream, which stands for "input-output stream." It's a standard C++ library that allows you to perform input and output operations, such as printing to the screen.
- int main() { ... }: This is the main function of your program. Every C++ program must have a main function. It's where the program starts executing. The curly braces { ... } contain the code that will be executed when the program runs.
- // Your code goes here: This is a comment. Comments are ignored by the computer but provide information to the programmer (you). It's good practice to add comments to explain your code.
- return 0;: This line signifies the end of the main function. The return 0; statement indicates that the program has executed successfully. A non-zero value here usually indicates an error.

## Writing Your First Program

Let's create a simple "Hello, World!" program, which is a traditional starting point for learning any programming language. In this program, we'll make the computer display the text "Hello, World!" on the screen.

```cpp
#include <iostream>

int main() {
    // Print "Hello, World!" to the screen
    std::cout << "Hello, World!" << std::endl;

    return 0;
}
```

Here's what's happening in this program:

- #include <iostream>: We include the iostream library.
- int main() { ... }: We define the main function.
- std::cout << "Hello, World!" << std::endl;: This line is responsible for printing "Hello, World!" to the screen. std::cout represents the standard output (the screen), and << is used to output the text. std::endl is used to end the line, moving the cursor to the next line.

## Compiling and Running Your Program

Now that you've written your first C++ program, it's time to compile and run it. Here's how:

1. Save your program with a .cpp file extension, such as hello.cpp.
2. Open a command prompt or terminal window.
3. Navigate to the directory where you saved your program.
4. Compile the program using a C++ compiler. For example, if you're using the GNU Compiler Collection (GCC), you can compile the program with the following command:

```
g++ hello.cpp -o hello
```

This command tells the compiler to take your hello.cpp file and produce an executable named hello.

5. Run the program by typing:

```
./hello
```

You should see the output "Hello, World!" displayed on the screen.

Congratulations! You've successfully written, compiled, and run your first C++ program. You're now officially a C++ programmer. In the chapters that follow, we'll explore C++ in more depth, covering variables, data types, control structures, and many other essential concepts.

# 1.3 Compiling and Running C++ Code

In the previous section, you learned how to write a simple C++ program that displayed "Hello, World!" on the screen. Now, let's explore the process of compiling and running your C++ code, which is a crucial step in the software development workflow.

**The Compilation Process**

When you write C++ code, the computer doesn't understand it directly. It needs a translation from the human-readable code you wrote into machine-executable instructions. This translation is done by a **C++ compiler**. The compiler checks your code for syntax errors and converts it into a format that can be executed by the computer's CPU.

*Compiling with g++*

One commonly used C++ compiler is **g++**, part of the GNU Compiler Collection (GCC). To compile a C++ program using g++, follow these steps:

1. **Open a Terminal or Command Prompt:** Depending on your operating system, open a terminal window or command prompt.
2. **Navigate to the Program's Directory:** Use the cd (change directory) command to navigate to the directory where your C++ program is saved. For example:

```
cd /path/to/your/program
```

3. **Compile the Program:** Use the g++ command followed by the name of your C++ source file (with a .cpp extension) and the -o flag to specify the name of the output executable. For example:

```
g++ hello.cpp -o hello
```

In this command, hello.cpp is the name of your source file, and hello is the name of the executable program that will be created.

4. **Run the Executable:** After a successful compilation, you can run your program by entering:

```
./hello
```

You should see the output of your program displayed on the screen.

### Understanding Compilation Errors

While writing code, it's common to make mistakes. These can include syntax errors, typographical errors, or logic errors. When you compile your code, the compiler checks for such errors and reports them if found.

Here are a few common types of errors you might encounter during compilation:

- **Syntax Errors:** These occur when you violate the rules of the C++ language, such as missing semicolons, mismatched parentheses, or undefined variables.
- **Typographical Errors:** Simple mistakes like misspelled variable or function names can lead to compilation errors.
- **Linker Errors:** These occur when the compiler can't find a reference to a function or variable used in your code.
- **Logic Errors:** These errors don't necessarily cause compilation failures, but they can lead to unexpected program behavior. They are often more challenging to identify and fix.

### Debugging and Iteration

Don't be discouraged by compilation errors; they are a natural part of the programming process. In fact, experienced programmers often say that "programming is 10% writing code and 90% debugging."

When you encounter an error, the compiler will usually provide a descriptive error message, including the line number where the error occurred. Use these messages as clues to identify and fix the problem in your code.

Remember that programming is an iterative process. You write code, test it, encounter errors, fix them, and repeat. Over time, you'll become more skilled at identifying and addressing issues, and your programs will become more robust.

## 1.4 Comments and Documentation

In the previous sections, you learned how to write your first C++ program, compile it, and run it. Now, let's explore an essential aspect of writing clean and maintainable code: comments and documentation.

## The Importance of Comments

Comments are non-executable lines of text within your code that are meant for human readers, including yourself and other programmers who may work on the code. They provide explanations, clarifications, and context about the code. Comments are crucial for the following reasons:

1. **Code Understanding:** Comments help you and others understand what the code is doing, why it's doing it, and how it's accomplishing its goals. This is especially valuable when revisiting your code after some time.
2. **Collaboration:** When you collaborate with other programmers on a project, comments act as a form of communication. They make it easier for team members to comprehend and work with your code.
3. **Debugging and Maintenance:** Comments can serve as breadcrumbs when debugging or maintaining code. They can help you pinpoint potential issues or understand the purpose of specific sections of code.

## Types of Comments

In C++, there are two primary ways to add comments to your code: single-line comments and multi-line comments.

### Single-Line Comments

Single-line comments start with two forward slashes (//) and continue until the end of the line. Anything following // is considered a comment and is ignored by the compiler. Here's an example:

```
// This is a single-line comment
int age = 30; // This is a comment at the
end of a line
```

*Multi-Line Comments*

Multi-line comments begin with /* and end with */. Anything between these delimiters is treated as a comment. Multi-line comments are useful when you want to add comments that span multiple lines:

```
/*
   This is a multi-line comment.
   It can span several lines and is often
used for detailed explanations.
*/
int x = 42;
```

## Best Practices for Writing Comments

Writing effective comments is an art that improves with practice. Here are some best practices to keep in mind:

1. **Be Clear and Concise:** Write comments that are easy to understand and get straight to the point. Avoid overly complex or cryptic comments.
2. **Use Comments Sparingly:** While comments are essential, strive for code that is self-explanatory. Well-named variables and clear code structure reduce the need for excessive comments.
3. **Update Comments:** Keep comments up to date as you modify your code. Outdated comments can mislead and cause confusion.
4. **Follow a Consistent Style:** Adhere to a consistent style for writing comments throughout your codebase. This makes the code more readable and professional.

## Documentation

While comments are essential for explaining individual pieces of code, documentation provides a higher-level overview of your entire program or project. Documentation often includes information about how to use your code, its purpose, and any dependencies or requirements.

Many C++ projects use documentation tools like Doxygen or Javadoc to generate documentation from specially formatted comments in the code. These tools make it easier to maintain and publish comprehensive documentation for your code.

# 2: VARIABLES AND DATA TYPES

## 2.1 Introduction to Variables

In Chapter 1, you took your first steps in C++ by writing a simple "Hello, World!" program. While that program was straightforward, it didn't involve much manipulation of data. In this chapter, we'll introduce you to the concept of **variables**, which is fundamental to working with data in C++.

### What are Variables?

Variables are like named storage locations in a computer's memory. They allow you to store and manipulate data within your programs. Think of a variable as a container with a label. You can place data, such as numbers, text, or other values, into these containers and use them in your code.

Variables are essential because they enable your programs to remember and process information dynamically. Whether you're calculating the sum of two numbers, storing a user's name, or tracking the score in a game, variables are your go-to tool for working with data.

### Variable Names and Rules

In C++, variable names are identifiers that you create to represent your data. Here are some important rules and conventions for naming variables:

- Variable names can consist of letters, digits, and underscores.

- Variable names must start with a letter or an underscore.
- Variable names are case-sensitive. For example, myVariable and myvariable are considered different variables.
- Avoid using C++ reserved keywords (e.g., int, while, if) as variable names.
- Use descriptive and meaningful names that indicate the purpose of the variable. For example, use totalPrice instead of x to represent the total price of items in a shopping cart.

Here's an example of declaring and initializing a variable in C++:

```
int age;           // Declaration: Tells the
compiler we will have a variable named 'age'
of type int.
age = 30;          // Initialization: Assigns
the value 30 to the 'age' variable.
```

## Data Types

Variables in C++ must have a **data type**, which specifies the kind of data that can be stored in the variable and the operations that can be performed on it. C++ provides several built-in data types, each designed to handle different types of data:

- **int:** Used for integers (whole numbers) like -42, 0, or 100.
- **double:** Used for floating-point numbers (numbers with decimal points) like 3.14 or -0.005.
- **char:** Used for single characters like 'A' or '5'.
- **bool:** Used for boolean values, which are either true or false.

Choosing the right data type for your variables is crucial because it affects memory usage, performance, and the range of values the variable can hold.

## Your First Variable

Let's write your first C++ program that uses variables. We'll declare a variable, assign a value to it, and then display that value on the screen. This simple example will demonstrate the practical use of variables and set the stage for more complex data manipulations in the chapters ahead.

```cpp
#include <iostream>

int main() {
    // Declare an integer variable named
'age' and initialize it with a value
    int age = 30;

    // Display the value of the 'age'
variable
    std::cout << "My age is: " << age <<
std::endl;

    return 0;
}
```

In this program, we've declared an integer variable named age, initialized it with the value 30, and then printed that value to the screen using std::cout.

## 2.2 Data Types in C++

In the previous section, you were introduced to variables, which serve as containers for storing and manipulating data within your programs. In C++, each variable must have a **data type** that specifies the kind of data it can hold. C++ provides several built-in data types to handle different types of values and operations.

**Common Data Types**

Here are some of the most commonly used data types in C++:

*1. int (Integer):*

- Represents whole numbers, both positive and negative.
- Example: int age = 30;

*2. double (Double Precision Floating-Point):*

- Represents real numbers with decimal points.
- Example: double pi = 3.14159;

*3. char (Character):*

- Represents a single character enclosed in single quotes.
- Example: char grade = 'A';

*4. bool (Boolean):*

- Represents either true or false.
- Example: bool isStudent = true;

## Modifiers and Qualifiers

C++ allows you to modify or qualify these basic data types to meet specific requirements. Here are some modifiers and qualifiers:

*1. unsigned:*

- Used with int and char data types.
- Restricts variables to non-negative values (zero or positive).
- Example: unsigned int score = 95;

*2. short:*

- Used with int.
- Reduces the range of values that can be stored (usually 16 bits).
- Example: short temperature = -10;

*3. long:*

- Used with int.

- Increases the range of values that can be stored (usually 32 bits or more).
- Example: long population = 8000000;

*4. float (Single Precision Floating-Point):*

- Represents real numbers with decimal points (less precision compared to double).
- Example: float height = 5.8f;

*5. const:*

- Used to declare constants, which are values that cannot be changed after initialization.
- Example: const double gravity = 9.81;

**Choosing the Right Data Type**

Selecting the appropriate data type for your variables is crucial for efficient memory usage and accurate data representation. Here are some guidelines to help you choose:

- Use int for whole numbers unless you have specific requirements that necessitate a different type.
- Use double for most floating-point calculations to ensure precision.
- Use char for single characters or small sets of characters (e.g., 'A', 'b').
- Use bool for true/false values or conditions.

**Size and Range of Data Types**

The size (in bits) and range (minimum and maximum values) of data types can vary between different C++ implementations and systems. You can use the sizeof operator to determine the size of a data type on your system. For example:

```
#include <iostream>
```

```
int main() {
    std::cout << "Size of int: " <<
sizeof(int) << " bytes" << std::endl;
    std::cout << "Size of double: " <<
sizeof(double) << " bytes" << std::endl;
    std::cout << "Size of char: " <<
sizeof(char) << " bytes" << std::endl;
    std::cout << "Size of bool: " <<
sizeof(bool) << " bytes" << std::endl;

    return 0;
}
```

Keep in mind that while the size and range of data types may vary, the general principles and usage of these data types remain consistent across most C++ implementations.

**User-Defined Data Types**

In addition to the built-in data types, C++ allows you to create your own custom data types using **structures** and **classes**, which we'll explore in later chapters. These user-defined data types are powerful tools for organizing and encapsulating data and behavior in your programs.

# 2.3 Declaring and Initializing Variables

In C++, the process of creating a variable involves two essential steps: **declaration** and **initialization**.

Declaration of Variables

**Declaration** is the act of specifying the data type and name of a variable to inform the compiler about its existence. It tells the compiler to allocate memory for the variable of the specified type. Here's the basic syntax for declaring a variable:

```
data_type variable_name;
```

- data_type: Specifies the type of data the variable will hold (e.g., int, double, char, bool).
- variable_name: The name you give to the variable, following the naming rules and conventions.

For example, let's declare a few variables:

```
int age;          // Declaration of an
integer variable named 'age'
double price;     // Declaration of a double
variable named 'price'
char initial;     // Declaration of a
character variable named 'initial'
bool isStudent;   // Declaration of a
boolean variable named 'isStudent'
```

After declaration, variables exist in memory but do not have defined values. Their contents are undefined until you explicitly assign values to them.

### Initialization of Variables

**Initialization** is the process of assigning an initial value to a variable when it's declared. Initializing variables at the point of declaration is a good practice because it ensures that variables start with known and meaningful values. Here's the syntax for declaring and initializing a variable:

```
data_type variable_name = initial_value;
```

- data_type: The type of data the variable will hold.
- variable_name: The name of the variable.
- initial_value: The value assigned to the variable during initialization.

Here are some examples of variable declaration and initialization:

```
int age = 30;                        //
Declaration and initialization of 'age' with
the value 30
double price = 19.99;                //
Declaration and initialization of 'price'
with the value 19.99
char initial = 'A';                  //
Declaration and initialization of 'initial'
with the character 'A'
bool isStudent = true;               //
Declaration and initialization of
'isStudent' with the value true
```

It's important to note that variables can be declared without immediate initialization, but it's recommended to initialize them whenever possible to prevent using undefined values.

### Default Initialization

If you declare a variable without explicitly initializing it, C++ provides a default initialization value based on the variable's data type. However, relying on default initialization is not considered a best practice because it may lead to unexpected behavior. Always aim to initialize your variables explicitly.

Here's how variables are typically initialized when not explicitly specified:

- int: Default initializes to 0.
- double: Default initializes to 0.0.
- char: Default initializes to the null character '\0'.
- bool: Default initializes to false.

### Multiple Variable Declarations

You can declare multiple variables of the same data type in a single declaration statement, separating them with commas:

```
int x, y, z;                  // Declaration
of three integer variables: x, y, and z
double width, height;         // Declaration
of two double variables: width and height
char first, last;             // Declaration
of two character variables: first and last
```

This can help you organize related variables conveniently.

**Variable Reassignment**

After initializing a variable, you can change its value by assigning a new value using the assignment operator (=). For example:

```
int age = 30;      // Initialize 'age' with
30
age = 31;          // Reassign 'age' with
31
```

In this example, age is first initialized with the value 30 and then reassigned to the value 31.

As you work on your C++ programs, mastering variable declaration and initialization is crucial. It sets the stage for manipulating and using data effectively within your code.

# 2.4 Constants

In programming, there are values that should never change throughout the execution of a program. These unchanging values are called **constants**. Constants are used to represent fixed values, such as mathematical constants (e.g., $\pi$), physical constants (e.g., the speed of light), or configuration settings that should remain unchanged during the program's execution.

In C++, you can define constants using the const keyword. Constants provide several advantages, including code readability and the prevention of accidental changes to important values.

## Declaring Constants

To declare a constant in C++, you use the const keyword followed by the data type, a name for the constant, and an initializer. Here's the basic syntax:

```
const data_type constant_name =
initial_value;
```

- const: Indicates that the variable is a constant and cannot be modified after initialization.
- data_type: Specifies the type of data the constant will hold (e.g., int, double, char, bool).
- constant_name: The name you give to the constant, following naming rules and conventions.
- initial_value: The initial value assigned to the constant.

Here are some examples of constant declarations:

```
const double pi = 3.14159;          //
Declaration of a constant 'pi' with the
value 3.14159
const int daysInWeek = 7;           //
Declaration of a constant 'daysInWeek' with
the value 7
const char newline = '\n';          //
Declaration of a constant 'newline' with the
newline character
const bool isDebugMode = false;     //
Declaration of a constant 'isDebugMode' with
the value false
```

Once declared and initialized, a constant's value cannot be changed. Attempting to do so will result in a compilation error.

## Advantages of Constants

Constants offer several benefits in programming:

1. **Readability:** Constants make your code more readable by giving meaningful names to fixed values. For example, using const int daysInWeek = 7; is more descriptive than simply using the number 7 throughout your code.
2. **Safety:** Constants prevent accidental modification of critical values. If you use a constant for a value that should remain constant, any attempt to change it will result in a compiler error, alerting you to the mistake.
3. **Maintenance:** When you need to change a constant value that appears multiple times in your code, you only need to update it in one place, making maintenance easier and reducing the risk of errors.

## Using Constants in Expressions

Constants can be used in expressions just like regular variables. They contribute to code clarity and help you avoid "magic numbers," which are unexplained numeric values that appear in your code.

For example, consider this code snippet:

```
const double taxRate = 0.08; // Assume a tax
rate of 8%

double purchaseAmount = 100.0;
double totalTax = purchaseAmount * taxRate;
double totalPrice = purchaseAmount +
totalTax;
```

In this code, taxRate is a constant that represents the tax rate. Using this constant makes it clear that the tax rate is 8%, and you don't need to use the literal value 0.08 throughout your code.

## Enumeration Constants

In addition to using the const keyword, you can define constants using **enumerations** (enum), which create a set of named integer constants. Enumerations are particularly useful when you need to represent a set of related constant values.

Here's an example of an enumeration for days of the week:

```
enum DaysOfWeek {
    Sunday,
    Monday,
    Tuesday,
    Wednesday,
    Thursday,
    Friday,
    Saturday
};
```

In this enumeration, Sunday is assigned the value 0, Monday is 1, and so on. Enumerations provide a way to create a collection of named constants for better code organization.

## 2.5 Type Conversion

In C++, variables have specific data types that define the kind of data they can hold and the operations that can be performed on them. Sometimes, you may need to convert a variable from one data type to another, either to perform a specific operation or to store it in a different format. This process is known as **type conversion** or **type casting**.

**Implicit Type Conversion (Coercion)**

C++ performs automatic type conversion, known as **implicit type conversion** or **coercion**, under certain circumstances. This happens when the compiler automatically converts a value from one data type to another, typically when it's safe to do so without loss of data or precision.

Here are a few common scenarios of implicit type conversion:

1. **Promotion:** When a smaller data type is converted to a larger data type. For example, converting an int to a double.

2. **Mixed Expressions:** When you perform operations involving variables of different data types, the result may be automatically converted to a compatible type.

```
int num1 = 5;
double num2 = 3.14;
double result = num1 + num2; // Implicit
conversion of 'num1' to 'double'
```

3. **Assignment:** When you assign a value of one data type to a variable of another data type, and the conversion is safe.

```
int intValue = 42;
double doubleValue = intValue; // Implicit
conversion of 'intValue' to 'double'
```

Explicit Type Conversion (Casting)

In cases where you need to explicitly convert a variable from one data type to another, you can use **explicit type conversion** or **casting**. C++ provides two primary ways to perform explicit type conversion:

1. **C-Style Type Casting:**

   This involves placing the desired data type in parentheses before the value to be converted. It's often referred to as a C-style cast.

```
double pi = 3.14159;
int intPi = (int)pi; // C-style casting:
Convert 'pi' to an integer (truncates
decimal part)
```

2. **C++ Type Casting Operators:**

   C++ provides specific casting operators for more controlled type conversions. These operators are considered safer and more readable than C-style casting. The three primary C++ casting operators are:

o static_cast: Used for general type conversions.
o dynamic_cast: Used for conversions in the context of polymorphism (e.g., casting between base and derived classes).
o reinterpret_cast: Used for low-level bit manipulation.

Here's an example of using static_cast for explicit type conversion:

```
double pi = 3.14159;
int intPi = static_cast<int>(pi); // Using
static_cast to convert 'pi' to an integer
```

**Beware of Data Loss**

When performing type conversion, especially when converting from a larger data type to a smaller one (e.g., double to int), be aware that you may lose data or precision. In such cases, the value is typically truncated or rounded down.

For example:

```
double value = 3.99;
int intValue = static_cast<int>(value); //
intValue will be 3, not 3.99
```

**Type Conversion in Practice**

Type conversion is a powerful tool that allows you to work with data in different formats and perform a wide range of operations. However, it's important to use it carefully and with a clear understanding of the implications. Improper type conversion can lead to unexpected results and errors in your programs.

# 3: OPERATORS AND EXPRESSIONS

## 3.1 Arithmetic Operators

Arithmetic operators are fundamental tools in programming that allow you to perform basic mathematical operations on numeric data types. C++ provides a set of standard arithmetic operators that enable you to perform addition, subtraction, multiplication, division, and more.

**Addition + Operator**

The addition operator (+) is used to add two values together. It works with both integers and floating-point numbers.

```
int sum = 5 + 3;        // Adds 5 and 3,
result is 8
double total = 2.5 + 3.7; // Adds 2.5 and
3.7, result is 6.2
```

**Subtraction - Operator**

The subtraction operator (-) is used to subtract the right operand from the left operand. It can also work with both integers and floating-point numbers.

```
int difference = 10 - 4;   // Subtracts 4
from 10, result is 6
```

```
double result = 7.5 - 2.2; // Subtracts 2.2
from 7.5, result is 5.3
```

## Multiplication * Operator

The multiplication operator (*) is used to multiply two values together. It can be used with both integers and floating-point numbers.

```
int product = 6 * 7;         // Multiplies 6
and 7, result is 42
double area = 3.14 * 5.0; // Multiplies π
(approximated as 3.14) and 5.0, result is
15.7
```

## Division / Operator

The division operator (/) is used to divide the left operand by the right operand. It can yield a quotient with or without decimals, depending on the data types of the operands.

```
int quotient = 20 / 4;         // Divides 20 by
4, result is 5 (integer division)
double result = 10.0 / 3.0; // Divides 10.0
by 3.0, result is 3.3333... (floating-point
division)
```

## Modulus % Operator

The modulus operator (%) is used to find the remainder when one number is divided by another. It is often used to check for divisibility or to cycle through a range of values.

```
int remainder = 15 % 4; // Finds the
remainder when 15 is divided by 4, result is
3
```

## Operator Precedence

When multiple operators are used in a single expression, they are evaluated in a specific order, known as operator precedence. Arithmetic operators follow the typical order of operations:

1. Parentheses (): Operations within parentheses are evaluated first.
2. Multiplication * and Division /: These operators are evaluated next, from left to right.
3. Addition + and Subtraction -: These operators are evaluated last, also from left to right.

You can use parentheses to override the default order of evaluation and ensure that specific operations are performed first.

```
int result = (5 + 3) * 2; // Uses
parentheses to ensure addition is performed
before multiplication
```

## Mixed Data Types

When using arithmetic operators with operands of different data types, C++ performs implicit type conversion to ensure that the operands have compatible types for the operation. The result of such an operation will typically have the higher-precision data type of the operands.

```
int intValue = 5;
double doubleValue = 2.5;
double result = intValue + doubleValue; //
intValue is implicitly converted to double
```

Arithmetic operators are the building blocks of mathematical computations in C++. Understanding how to use them effectively is essential for performing calculations and manipulating numeric data in your programs.

## 3.2 Relational and Logical Operators

Relational and logical operators are fundamental tools in C++ that enable you to create expressions for making decisions, comparisons, and evaluating conditions. These operators are essential for controlling the flow of your programs and determining the outcome of various operations.

**Relational Operators**

Relational operators are used to compare two values and determine the relationship between them. They return a Boolean value (true or false) based on the comparison result. Here are the common relational operators in C++:

- **Equality (==):** Checks if two values are equal.
- **Inequality (!=):** Checks if two values are not equal.
- **Greater Than (>):** Checks if the left operand is greater than the right operand.
- **Less Than (<):** Checks if the left operand is less than the right operand.
- **Greater Than or Equal To (>=):** Checks if the left operand is greater than or equal to the right operand.
- **Less Than or Equal To (<=):** Checks if the left operand is less than or equal to the right operand.

Here are some examples of how these operators are used:

```
int x = 5;
int y = 10;

bool isEqual = (x == y);      // false (5 is
not equal to 10)
bool isNotEqual = (x != y);   // true (5 is
not equal to 10)
bool isGreaterThan = (x > y); // false (5 is
not greater than 10)
```

```
bool isLessThan = (x < y);    // true (5 is
less than 10)
```

**Logical Operators**

Logical operators are used to combine multiple conditions or Boolean values to form more complex conditions. They allow you to create expressions that evaluate to either true or false based on the logical relationship between the operands. Here are the common logical operators in C++:

- **Logical AND (&&):** Returns true if both operands are true.
- **Logical OR (||):** Returns true if at least one of the operands is true.
- **Logical NOT (!):** Negates the value of the operand; if it's true, it becomes false, and vice versa.

Logical operators are often used in conditional statements (e.g., if, while, for) to control program flow based on specific conditions:

```
int age = 25;
bool isStudent = true;

if (age >= 18 && isStudent) {
    // Code to grant a student discount
}
```

In this example, the && (logical AND) operator is used to check if age is greater than or equal to 18 **and** isStudent is true before granting a student discount.

**Operator Precedence**

Relational and logical operators have a specific order of precedence when evaluating expressions. Relational operators have higher precedence than logical operators. However, you can use parentheses to control the order of evaluation, just as with arithmetic operators.

For example:

```
bool result = (x > 5) && (y <= 10);
```

In this expression, the parentheses ensure that the relational comparisons are performed first, and then the logical AND operation is applied to the results.

**Combining Operators**

You can combine multiple relational and logical operators to create complex conditions. This is particularly useful when you need to evaluate multiple criteria to make decisions or filter data:

```
int score = 75;
bool isPassing = (score >= 60) && (score <= 100);
```

In this example, isPassing is true if score is greater than or equal to 60 **and** less than or equal to 100, indicating that the student has passed.

## 3.3 Assignment Operators

Assignment operators are fundamental tools in C++ that allow you to assign values to variables. These operators are used to update the value of a variable, making it an essential part of variable manipulation in your programs.

**The Basic Assignment Operator (=)**

The most common assignment operator is the basic assignment operator (=). It is used to assign a value to a variable. Here's a simple example:

```
int age = 25; // Assigns the value 25 to the
variable 'age'
```

In this example, the value 25 is assigned to the variable age. After this assignment, the variable age holds the value 25.

## Compound Assignment Operators

C++ provides compound assignment operators that combine an operation with assignment. These operators allow you to update the value of a variable in a more concise way. Here are some common compound assignment operators:

- **Addition Assignment (+=):** Adds the right operand to the left operand and assigns the result to the left operand.

```
int num = 10;
num += 5; // Equivalent to num = num + 5,
updates 'num' to 15
```

- **Subtraction Assignment (-=):** Subtracts the right operand from the left operand and assigns the result to the left operand.

```
int total = 100;
total -= 20; // Equivalent to total = total
- 20, updates 'total' to 80
```

- **Multiplication Assignment (*=):** Multiplies the left operand by the right operand and assigns the result to the left operand.

```
int quantity = 4;
quantity *= 3; // Equivalent to quantity =
quantity * 3, updates 'quantity' to 12
```

- **Division Assignment (/=):** Divides the left operand by the right operand and assigns the result to the left operand.

```
int price = 60;
price /= 2; // Equivalent to price = price /
2, updates 'price' to 30
```

- **Modulus Assignment (%=):** Performs the modulus operation on the left operand using the right operand and assigns the result to the left operand.

```
int remainder = 15;
remainder %= 4; // Equivalent to remainder =
remainder % 4, updates 'remainder' to 3
```

Compound assignment operators are not only concise but also efficient because they can be optimized by the compiler.

## Chaining Assignment

C++ allows you to chain assignment operators together to perform multiple assignments in a single statement. This is particularly useful when initializing multiple variables with the same value.

```
int x, y, z;
x = y = z = 10; // Assigns the value 10 to
all three variables: x, y, and z
```

In this example, z is assigned the value 10, and then y and x are assigned the value of z, which is also 10.

## Use Case: Increment and Decrement

Compound assignment operators are commonly used with the increment (++) and decrement (--) operators to increase or decrease the value of a variable by one.

```
int count = 5;
count++; // Equivalent to count = count + 1,
updates 'count' to 6
count--; // Equivalent to count = count - 1,
updates 'count' to 5
```

You can also use the compound assignment operators with increment and decrement:

```
int num = 7;
num += 3; // Equivalent to num = num + 3,
updates 'num' to 10
num -= 2; // Equivalent to num = num - 2,
updates 'num' to 8
```

Assignment operators are essential for managing the values of variables in your C++ programs. Whether you're assigning initial values, updating variables based on conditions, or performing complex calculations, mastering assignment operators is crucial for effective variable manipulation.

## 3.4 Increment and Decrement Operators

Increment and decrement operators are specialized operators in C++ that are used to increase or decrease the value of a variable by one. These operators are commonly used for tasks such as counting, looping, and tracking positions within data structures.

**Increment Operator (++)**

The increment operator (++) is used to increase the value of a variable by one. It can be applied in two ways: **pre-increment** and **post-increment**.

1. **Pre-increment (++variable):** In pre-increment, the value of the variable is increased before its updated value is used in an expression.

```
int num = 5;
int result = ++num; // Pre-increment 'num'
by 1, then use the updated value
```

In this example, num is pre-incremented, so its value becomes 6, and result also becomes 6.

2. **Post-increment (variable++):** In post-increment, the current value of the variable is used in an expression before it is increased by one.

```
int num = 5;
int result = num++; // Use the current value
of 'num' and then post-increment it
```

In this case, num is post-incremented, so its value is used in the expression (resulting in 5), and then num is increased to 6.

Decrement Operator (--)

The decrement operator (--) is used to decrease the value of a variable by one, similar to the increment operator. It also has pre-decrement and post-decrement forms.

1. **Pre-decrement (--variable):** In pre-decrement, the value of the variable is decreased before its updated value is used in an expression.

```
int num = 8;
int result = --num; // Pre-decrement 'num'
by 1, then use the updated value
```

Here, num is pre-decremented, making its value 7, and result also becomes 7.

2. **Post-decrement (variable--):** In post-decrement, the current value of the variable is used in an expression before it is decreased by one.

```
int num = 8;
int result = num--; // Use the current value
of 'num' and then post-decrement it
```

In this case, num is post-decremented, so its value is used in the expression (resulting in 8), and then num is decreased to 7.

**Use Cases**

Increment and decrement operators are commonly used in various programming scenarios:

- **Looping:** They are frequently used in for and while loops to control iteration and modify loop variables.

```
for (int i = 0; i < 5; ++i) {
    // Loop code with 'i' ranging from 0 to 4
}
```

- **Counting:** They are used to keep track of counts, scores, or indices within arrays and data structures.

```
int count = 0;
count++; // Increment count by 1
```

- **Movement in Data Structures:** They can be used to move through arrays, linked lists, and other data structures.

```
int index = 0;
++index; // Move to the next element
```

Understanding when and how to use increment and decrement operators is essential for efficient and concise programming in C++. These operators play a significant role in controlling program flow and managing variables in various applications.

## 3.5 Expressions and Precedence

In C++, expressions are combinations of values, variables, operators, and function calls that yield a single result. Understanding how expressions are evaluated and the rules governing operator precedence is crucial for writing correct and efficient code.

## Expressions

An expression can be as simple as a single variable or as complex as a series of operations and function calls. Here are some examples of expressions:

- Simple variable reference: x
- Arithmetic expression: 5 + 3
- Combining variables and operators: a * b - c
- Using parentheses to control evaluation order: (x + y) / (a - b)
- Function call: calculateTotal(quantity, price)

Expressions are the foundation of programming logic in C++, as they allow you to perform calculations, make decisions, and manipulate data.

## Operator Precedence

In C++, operators have different levels of precedence, which determines the order in which they are evaluated within an expression. Understanding operator precedence is essential because it helps you predict how expressions will be evaluated and allows you to write code that behaves as expected.

Here's a general guideline for the precedence of common operators, from highest to lowest:

1. **Parentheses ():** Operations within parentheses are evaluated first. You can use parentheses to override the default precedence and specify the order of evaluation.
2. **Post-increment variable++ and Post-decrement variable--:** These have higher precedence than most other operators.
3. **Pre-increment ++variable and Pre-decrement --variable:** Like their post counterparts, they have higher precedence.
4. **Arithmetic Operators +, -, *, /, %:** These include addition, subtraction, multiplication, division, and modulus. They have typical mathematical precedence rules.

5. **Relational Operators <, <=, >, >=, ==, !=:** These are used for comparisons.
6. **Logical NOT !:** Negates the value of an expression.
7. **Logical AND &&:** Used to combine conditions with logical AND.
8. **Logical OR ||:** Used to combine conditions with logical OR.
9. **Assignment Operators =, +=, -= and others:** Assignment operators have lower precedence than most other operators.
10. **Comma ,:** Used to separate expressions and evaluate them from left to right.

It's essential to remember that operator precedence determines the order in which operators are evaluated. When expressions involve operators with different precedence levels, the operator with higher precedence is evaluated first.

### Example of Operator Precedence

Consider the following expression:

```
int result = 5 + 3 * 2 - 1;
```

The result of this expression is determined by operator precedence:

1. 3 * 2 is evaluated first due to the higher precedence of the * operator, resulting in 6.
2. 5 + 6 is evaluated next, using the + operator, resulting in 11.
3. Finally, 11 - 1 is evaluated, using the - operator, resulting in 10.

By understanding operator precedence, you can predict that result will hold the value 10.

### Parentheses for Control

While operator precedence is essential, you can always use parentheses to explicitly specify the order of evaluation, making your code more readable and avoiding potential confusion. For example:

```
int result = (5 + 3) * 2 - 1; // Parentheses
override operator precedence
```

In this case, the addition inside the parentheses is evaluated first, ensuring that result holds the value 14.

## Complex Expressions

In real-world programming, expressions can become quite complex, involving multiple operators and function calls. In such cases, it's helpful to use parentheses to clarify the order of evaluation and ensure the desired outcome.

```
double total = (calculateSubtotal(itemPrice)
* (1 + taxRate)) - discount;
```

Here, parentheses clearly indicate the order of operations, making the code more understandable.

# CONTROL FLOW

## 4.1 Conditional Statements (if, else if, else)

Conditional statements are a fundamental building block of programming that allow you to make decisions in your code. They enable your program to execute different sets of instructions based on specific conditions. In C++, conditional statements are primarily implemented using if, else if, and else constructs.

**The if Statement**

The if statement is used to execute a block of code only if a specified condition is true. It follows this general structure:

```cpp
if (condition) {
    // Code to be executed if the condition
is true
}
```

Here's an example:

```cpp
int age = 20;

if (age >= 18) {
    cout << "You are an adult." << endl;
}
```

In this example, the condition age >= 18 is evaluated. If it's true (which it is because age is 20), the code inside the if block is executed, and the message "You are an adult" is displayed.

**The** else **Clause**

Sometimes, you want to provide an alternative set of instructions to execute when the condition in the if statement is false. This is where the else clause comes into play. Here's how it works:

```
if (condition) {
    // Code to be executed if the condition
is true
} else {
    // Code to be executed if the condition
is false
}
```

Consider this example:

```
int age = 15;

if (age >= 18) {
    cout << "You are an adult." << endl;
} else {
    cout << "You are not yet an adult." <<
endl;
}
```

In this case, because age is 15, the condition in the if statement is false, and the code inside the else block is executed, displaying "You are not yet an adult."

**The** else if **Clause**

In situations where you have multiple conditions to check, you can use the else if clause to specify additional conditions to evaluate. The else if clause comes after the initial if statement and before the else clause (if present). Here's the structure:

```cpp
if (condition1) {
    // Code to be executed if condition1 is
true
} else if (condition2) {
    // Code to be executed if condition2 is
true
} else {
    // Code to be executed if none of the
conditions are true
}
```

Consider this example:

```cpp
int score = 75;

if (score >= 90) {
    cout << "You got an A." << endl;
} else if (score >= 80) {
    cout << "You got a B." << endl;
} else if (score >= 70) {
    cout << "You got a C." << endl;
} else {
    cout << "You need to improve." << endl;
}
```

In this example, the program checks the value of score against multiple conditions. Depending on the score, it prints an appropriate message. Because score is 75, it falls into the third condition, and "You got a C" is displayed.

**Nesting Conditional Statements**

Conditional statements can also be nested within one another, allowing for more complex decision-making. For example:

```cpp
int x = 10;
int y = 5;

if (x > y) {
```

```
    if (x % 2 == 0) {
        cout << "x is greater than y and
even." << endl;
    } else {
        cout << "x is greater than y but not
even." << endl;
    }
} else {
    cout << "x is not greater than y." <<
endl;
}
```

In this nested if statement, the program first checks if x is greater than y. If that condition is true, it then checks whether x is even or not.

Conditional statements are powerful tools for directing the flow of your program based on specific conditions. They allow your code to adapt and make decisions, providing a dynamic and interactive experience for users.

## 4.2 Switch Statements

In addition to if, else if, and else statements, C++ offers another powerful tool for controlling the flow of your program: the switch statement. switch statements provide an efficient and organized way to handle multiple cases based on the value of an expression. They are particularly useful when you have a single expression that can match one of several constant values.

**The** switch **Statement Syntax**

The basic syntax of a switch statement looks like this:

```
switch (expression) {
    case constant1:
        // Code to execute if expression
matches constant1
```

```
        break;
    case constant2:
        // Code to execute if expression
matches constant2
        break;
    // Additional case statements as needed
    default:
        // Code to execute if none of the
cases match the expression
}
```

Here's a breakdown of how the switch statement works:

- The switch keyword is followed by a set of parentheses containing an expression.
- The expression's value is compared to the constants specified in the case labels.
- If a case label matches the expression's value, the code inside that case block is executed, and the break statement terminates the switch statement's execution.
- If none of the case labels match the expression's value, the code inside the default block (if present) is executed. The default block is optional.

**Example of a switch Statement**

Let's look at an example using a switch statement to determine the day of the week based on a numeric code:

```
int dayCode = 3;
string dayOfWeek;

switch (dayCode) {
    case 1:
        dayOfWeek = "Monday";
        break;
    case 2:
        dayOfWeek = "Tuesday";
        break;
```

```
        case 3:
            dayOfWeek = "Wednesday";
            break;
        case 4:
            dayOfWeek = "Thursday";
            break;
        case 5:
            dayOfWeek = "Friday";
            break;
        case 6:
            dayOfWeek = "Saturday";
            break;
        case 7:
            dayOfWeek = "Sunday";
            break;
        default:
            dayOfWeek = "Invalid day code";
}

cout << "The day is: " << dayOfWeek << endl;
```

In this example, the switch statement evaluates the value of dayCode. If dayCode is 3, it matches the case 3 label, and "Wednesday" is assigned to dayOfWeek. The break statement then exits the switch statement. If dayCode does not match any of the case labels, the default block is executed, assigning "Invalid day code" to dayOfWeek.

**The break Statement**

The break statement is used to exit a switch statement and prevent the execution of subsequent case blocks. It is essential to include break statements after each case block to ensure that only the code for the matching case is executed. If break is omitted, execution will continue into subsequent cases until a break is encountered or the switch statement ends.

## Fall-Through Behavior

In some situations, you might intentionally want multiple case blocks to share the same code. This behavior is known as "fall-through." In C++, you can achieve fall-through by omitting the break statement at the end of a case block:

```
int month = 3;
string monthName;

switch (month) {
    case 1:
    case 2:
    case 3:
        monthName = "Winter";
        break;
    case 4:
    case 5:
    case 6:
        monthName = "Spring";
        break;
    // Additional cases for other seasons
    default:
        monthName = "Invalid month";
}
```

In this example, multiple case blocks for winter (January, February, and March) and spring (April, May, and June) share the same code.

## When to Use switch Statements

switch statements are most suitable when you have a single expression with many possible constant values to compare against. They are especially efficient when compared to a series of if, else if, and else statements, as they directly jump to the relevant case.

However, switch statements have limitations:

- They can only compare against constant values (integers, characters, or enumerated types).
- They don't support complex conditions or ranges.
- They cannot be used for string comparisons directly (C++17 and later versions allow string comparisons with std::string using if and else if).

## 4.3 Loops (while, for, do-while)

Loops are essential control flow structures in programming that allow you to execute a block of code repeatedly. They are used when you need to perform tasks multiple times or iterate over a collection of data. In C++, there are three primary types of loops: while, for, and do-while. Each type has its own use cases and syntax.

**The while Loop**

The while loop is the most basic type of loop in C++. It repeats a block of code as long as a specified condition remains true. Here's the basic syntax:

```
while (condition) {
    // Code to execute while the condition
is true
}
```

For example, let's use a while loop to count from 1 to 5:

```
int count = 1;

while (count <= 5) {
    cout << count << " ";
    count++;
}

// Output: 1 2 3 4 5
```

In this example, the while loop checks the condition count <= 5. As long as the condition is true, it executes the code inside the loop, increments count, and continues until count becomes greater than 5.

**The for Loop**

The for loop is another common loop type in C++. It is especially useful when you know the number of iterations in advance. Here's the syntax:

```
for (initialization; condition; update) {
    // Code to execute while the condition
is true
}
```

Let's use a for loop to accomplish the same counting task:

```
for (int count = 1; count <= 5; count++) {
    cout << count << " ";
}

// Output: 1 2 3 4 5
```

In this for loop, the initialization (int count = 1), condition (count <= 5), and update (count++) are all defined within the loop header. The loop executes as long as the condition is true, which means it runs from count = 1 to count = 5.

**The do-while Loop**

The do-while loop is a variation of the while loop, but with one key difference: it guarantees that the loop body is executed at least once, even if the condition is initially false. Here's the syntax:

```
do {
    // Code to execute at least once
} while (condition);
```

Here's an example of using a do-while loop to obtain user input until they enter a positive number:

```
int userInput;
do {
    cout << "Enter a positive number: ";
    cin >> userInput;
} while (userInput <= 0);
```

In this case, the loop body executes at least once because the condition userInput <= 0 is evaluated after the code block. If the user enters a negative number or zero, the loop continues to prompt for input.

## Loop Control Statements

Loops can be further controlled using loop control statements:

- break: Terminates the loop prematurely and jumps to the code immediately following the loop.
- continue: Skips the rest of the current iteration and proceeds to the next iteration.
- return: Exits the entire function and, if applicable, the loop.

These control statements can be used to fine-tune the behavior of loops and make your code more efficient and readable.

## Choosing the Right Loop

The choice of which loop to use depends on the specific requirements of your task:

- Use a while loop when you need to repeat a block of code based on a condition, and you don't know the exact number of iterations in advance.
- Use a for loop when you have a fixed number of iterations, and you want to keep the loop control variables within the loop header.

- Use a do-while loop when you want to ensure that the loop body is executed at least once, regardless of the initial condition.

## 4.4 Break and Continue Statements

In C++, the break and continue statements are essential tools for controlling the flow of loops. They allow you to manipulate loops to break out of them prematurely or skip specific iterations based on certain conditions. These statements enhance the flexibility and efficiency of your code.

**The** break **Statement**

The break statement is used to exit a loop prematurely, regardless of whether the loop's termination condition is met. It is often used when a certain condition is satisfied, and you want to immediately exit the loop. Here's how it works:

```
while (condition) {
    // Code before the break statement

    if (condition_to_exit) {
        break; // Exit the loop
    }

    // Code after the break statement
}
```

For example, consider a while loop that searches for a specific element in an array and breaks when it finds the element:

```
int target = 42;
int numbers[] = {10, 20, 30, 42, 50, 60};
bool found = false;

for (int i = 0; i < 6; i++) {
    if (numbers[i] == target) {
```

```
        found = true;
        break; // Exit the loop when the
target is found
    }
}

if (found) {
    cout << "Target found!" << endl;
} else {
    cout << "Target not found." << endl;
}
```

In this example, the break statement is used to exit the loop as soon as the target is found. It prevents unnecessary iterations after the condition is met, improving efficiency.

**The continue Statement**

The continue statement, on the other hand, is used to skip the current iteration of a loop and move to the next iteration. It is particularly useful when you want to avoid executing certain code for specific iterations. Here's how it works:

```
while (condition) {
    // Code before the continue statement

    if (condition_to_skip) {
        continue; // Skip the rest of the
current iteration and move to the next
    }

    // Code after the continue statement
}
```

For example, let's use a for loop to print all even numbers from 1 to 10, skipping odd numbers:

```
for (int i = 1; i <= 10; i++) {
    if (i % 2 != 0) {
```

```
        continue; // Skip odd numbers
    }
    cout << i << " ";
}

// Output: 2 4 6 8 10
```

In this example, the continue statement is used to skip printing odd numbers. When i is odd, the loop moves to the next iteration without executing the cout statement.

**Use Cases**

- break is often used when you need to exit a loop early, such as when a specific condition is met or when you've found the desired result.
- continue is useful when you want to skip certain iterations, optimizing the execution of your loop by avoiding unnecessary computations.

Both break and continue statements should be used judiciously to maintain code clarity and readability. When used appropriately, they can simplify complex loops and improve the efficiency of your programs.

# 5: FUNCTIONS

## 5.1 Introduction to Functions

Functions are the building blocks of code organization and reusability in C++. They are an essential concept in programming that allows you to encapsulate a specific set of instructions into a self-contained unit, which can be invoked (called) whenever needed. Functions provide modularity to your code, making it easier to read, understand, and maintain.

**Why Use Functions?**

Functions serve several important purposes in programming:

1. **Modularity:** Functions allow you to break down your code into smaller, manageable pieces. Each function can focus on a specific task or functionality, making your code easier to understand.
2. **Reusability:** Once you've defined a function, you can call it multiple times from different parts of your program. This eliminates the need to duplicate code, reduces errors, and saves development time.
3. **Abstraction:** Functions provide a level of abstraction. When you call a function, you don't need to know the intricate details of how it works; you only need to understand its purpose and how to use it.
4. **Organization:** Functions help you organize your code logically. They enable you to structure your program into

smaller, meaningful sections, improving code readability and maintainability.

**Anatomy of a Function**

A C++ function consists of several components:

- **Return Type:** Every function has a return type, which specifies the type of value the function will return when it completes its task. If a function doesn't return a value, it uses the void return type.
- **Function Name:** A function is identified by its name, which should be unique within the scope of your program.
- **Parameters (Optional):** Functions can accept input data called parameters or arguments. Parameters are like placeholders that allow you to pass values into the function for processing.
- **Function Body:** The function body contains a set of statements enclosed in curly braces {}. These statements define what the function does when called.

Here's a basic syntax template for a function:

```
return_type function_name(parameters) {
    // Function body
}
```

**Example of a Simple Function**

Let's look at a simple function that calculates the square of a number and returns the result:

```
#include <iostream>

// Function declaration
int calculateSquare(int number);

int main() {
    int input = 5;
    int result = calculateSquare(input);
```

```
    std::cout << "The square of " << input
<< " is: " << result << std::endl;

    return 0;
}

// Function definition
int calculateSquare(int number) {
    return number * number;
}
```

In this example:

- We declare a function called calculateSquare with an int return type and one parameter, number.
- In the main function, we call calculateSquare with an input of 5.
- Inside calculateSquare, we perform the calculation and return the result.
- The result is printed in the main function.

Functions provide a structured way to organize and reuse code in your C++ programs. As you explore functions further, you'll discover more advanced features, such as function overloading, recursion, and working with libraries of pre-defined functions. These skills will empower you to build complex and modular applications efficiently.

## 5.2 Function Declaration and Definition

In C++, functions are typically declared and defined in separate parts of your code. Understanding how to declare and define functions correctly is essential for organizing your code and making it more readable and maintainable.

Function Declaration

A function declaration is a statement that tells the compiler about the existence and signature (return type, name, and parameter list) of a function. Function declarations are essential because they allow you to use a function before its actual definition in your code. This is particularly useful when you have functions calling each other or when you want to define functions in different parts of your code.

Here's the syntax for a function declaration:

```
return_type function_name(parameters);
```

- return_type: Specifies the data type of the value the function will return (use void if the function doesn't return a value).
- function_name: The name of the function, which must be unique within its scope.
- parameters: The list of input parameters (if any) that the function expects, enclosed in parentheses. If the function doesn't take any parameters, you should use empty parentheses ().

Here's an example of a function declaration:

```
int add(int a, int b); // Function
declaration
```

In this declaration, we inform the compiler that there's a function named add that takes two int parameters (a and b) and returns an int.

Function Definition

A function definition provides the actual implementation of the function. It specifies what the function does when called. Function definitions include the function's return type, name, parameter list, and the code block (function body) that contains the statements to be executed.

Here's the syntax for a function definition:

```
return_type function_name(parameters) {
    // Function body
    // Statements to be executed
    return value; // (if the function
returns a value)
}
```

- return_type: The same return type declared in the function declaration.
- function_name: The same function name declared in the function declaration.
- parameters: The same parameter list declared in the function declaration.
- function body: The set of statements to be executed when the function is called.
- return value: If the function returns a value, use the return statement to specify the value to be returned.

Here's an example of a function definition for the previously declared add function:

```
int add(int a, int b) {
    int sum = a + b;
    return sum;
}
```

In this definition, we provide the actual implementation of the add function. When called with two integers a and b, it calculates their sum and returns the result.

**Putting It All Together**

To use a function in your program, you need both a declaration and a definition. Here's how it works:

1. You declare the function to inform the compiler about its existence and signature.
2. You define the function to provide its implementation.

3.  You call the function in your code to execute the statements within its body.

Here's an example of how to declare, define, and use the add function:

```cpp
#include <iostream>

// Function declaration
int add(int a, int b);

int main() {
    // Function call
    int result = add(5, 3);
    std::cout << "The sum is: " << result << std::endl;

    return 0;
}

// Function definition
int add(int a, int b) {
    int sum = a + b;
    return sum;
}
```

By following this structure, you can create organized and modular code with reusable functions, improving the readability and maintainability of your C++ programs.

## 5.3 Function Parameters and Return Values

Functions in C++ can take input values, process them, and optionally return a result. Understanding how to work with function parameters and return values is fundamental to building versatile and modular code.

## Function Parameters

Function parameters (also called arguments) are values that are passed into a function when it is called. These values are used as input for the function's operations. Parameters are declared in the function's parameter list within the parentheses during both function declaration and definition.

### Declaring Parameters

In the function declaration, you specify the parameter names and their data types. Here's an example:

```
int add(int a, int b); // Declaration with
two parameters
```

In this declaration, add is a function that takes two int parameters, a and b.

### Defining Parameters

When defining the function, you include the parameter names and their data types again. These names act as placeholders for the values that will be passed into the function. Here's an example:

```
int add(int a, int b) {
    // Function body that uses 'a' and 'b'
    int sum = a + b;
    return sum;
}
```

In this definition, a and b are the parameters that receive the values when the function is called.

*Using Parameters*

To use the parameters within the function, you treat them like variables. In the example above, a and b are used to calculate the sum of two numbers.

**Function Return Values**

A function can also return a value to the caller. The return value is specified by the function's return type (e.g., int, double, string, or any other data type). The return statement is used to send a value back to the caller.

*Declaring Return Type*

In the function declaration, you specify the return type. If the function doesn't return a value, you use void as the return type. Here are examples of function declarations with different return types:

```
int add(int a, int b);        // Function
returns an integer.
double calculateAverage(int data[], int
size); // Function returns a double.
void displayMessage();        // Function
doesn't return a value (void).
```

*Returning Values*

In the function definition, you use the return statement to send a value back to the caller. The returned value should match the function's declared return type. Here's an example:

```
int add(int a, int b) {
    int sum = a + b;
    return sum; // Return the calculated sum
}
```

In this function, the return statement sends back the sum of a and b to the caller, which can then be assigned to a variable or used in an expression.

### Function Calls with Parameters and Return Values

When you call a function that has parameters and returns a value, you provide arguments (values) for the parameters, and you can capture the returned value. Here's an example of calling the add function:

```
int result = add(5, 3); // Calling 'add'
with arguments 5 and 3
```

In this call, 5 and 3 are passed as arguments to the add function. The result of the function (the sum) is then stored in the result variable.

### Multiple Parameters and Multiple Return Values

Functions can have multiple parameters, allowing you to pass in multiple values for processing. Similarly, you can return multiple values by using various techniques, such as returning a struct or using output parameters.

## 5.4 Function Overloading

Function overloading is a powerful feature in C++ that allows you to define multiple functions with the same name but different parameter lists. These functions can have the same or different return types. Function overloading enhances code flexibility by enabling you to create functions that perform similar tasks with varying input types or numbers of parameters.

### Overloaded Function Signatures

Function overloading is based on the concept of function signatures, which includes the function's name and its parameter list. Two functions with the same name and different parameter lists are considered overloaded.

*Example of Overloaded Functions*

Here's an example of overloaded functions for calculating the area of different shapes:

```
// Function to calculate the area of a
rectangle
double calculateArea(double length, double
width) {
    return length * width;
}

// Function to calculate the area of a
circle
double calculateArea(double radius) {
    return 3.14159265358979323846 * radius *
radius;
}
```

In this example, we have two functions named calculateArea, but they take different types and numbers of parameters. The first function calculates the area of a rectangle, while the second calculates the area of a circle.

**Function Overloading Rules**

To successfully overload functions, you must follow these rules:

1. Functions must have the same name.
2. Functions must differ in the number of parameters, or the data types of their parameters, or both.
3. Return types can be the same or different.

**Determining the Correct Function**

When you call an overloaded function, the C++ compiler determines which function to execute based on the number and types of arguments you pass during the function call. This process is called "function resolution" or "function matching."

Here's an example of calling the overloaded calculateArea functions:

```
double rectangleArea = calculateArea(5.0,
3.0); // Calls the rectangle area function
double circleArea = calculateArea(2.5);
// Calls the circle area function
```

In the first call, the function with two double parameters is matched, while in the second call, the function with a single double parameter is matched.

**Benefits of Function Overloading**

Function overloading offers several benefits:

1. **Improved Code Readability:** Overloaded functions provide a clear and concise way to handle different scenarios with the same function name.
2. **Code Reusability:** You can reuse a function name for similar tasks, reducing the need for creating distinct function names for each variation.
3. **Simplified Interfaces:** Overloading allows you to provide a consistent and user-friendly interface to clients of your code, making it easier for them to use your functions.

**Limitations**

While function overloading is a powerful feature, it has limitations:

1. **Function Ambiguity:** Care must be taken to avoid situations where the compiler cannot determine which overloaded function to call due to ambiguous parameter types.
2. **Return Type Alone Is Insufficient:** Overloaded functions must differ in their parameter lists, not just in return types. Overloading based solely on return type is not supported.

## Common Use Cases

Common use cases for function overloading include:

- Providing default arguments for functions.
- Handling different numeric types (e.g., int, double) for mathematical operations.
- Creating versatile input/output functions.

Function overloading is a valuable tool in your programming arsenal, enabling you to write clean, maintainable code that can handle a variety of scenarios with ease.

# 5.5 Scope and Lifetime of Variables

In C++, the scope and lifetime of variables are important concepts that determine where a variable can be accessed and for how long it remains in memory. Understanding these concepts is crucial when working with functions, as they affect how variables are used and managed within functions.

## Scope of Variables

The scope of a variable defines where in your code the variable is visible and can be accessed. In C++, there are primarily three types of variable scope:

1. **Local Scope (Function Scope):** Variables declared inside a function, including function parameters, have local scope. They are only accessible within that function and are not visible outside of it.

```
void myFunction() {
    int localVar = 10; // localVar has local
scope
}
```

2. **Block Scope:** Variables declared inside a block (within curly braces {}) have block scope. They are only accessible within that block and its nested blocks.

```
if (condition) {
    int blockVar = 5; // blockVar has block
scope
}
```

3. **Global Scope:** Variables declared outside of any function or block have global scope. They are accessible from any part of the code, including other functions.

```
int globalVar = 100; // globalVar has
global scope

void anotherFunction() {
    // globalVar is accessible here
}
```

**Lifetime of Variables**

The lifetime of a variable determines the period during which the variable exists in memory and retains its value. In C++, variables have one of the following lifetimes:

1. **Automatic (Local) Lifetime:** Variables with automatic storage duration, such as local variables declared inside a function, have a lifetime that begins when the function is called and ends when the function exits. They are created on the stack and are automatically destroyed when they go out of scope.

```
void myFunction() {
    int localVar = 10; // Automatic lifetime
(local variable)
} // localVar is destroyed here
```

2. **Static Lifetime:** Variables with static storage duration have a lifetime that extends throughout the entire program

execution. They are created and initialized only once, regardless of how many times the function containing them is called. Static variables are stored in a special area of memory called the "data segment."

```cpp
void myFunction() {
    static int staticVar = 5; // Static
lifetime
} // staticVar retains its value across
function calls
```

3. **Dynamic Lifetime:** Variables created dynamically using pointers, such as those created with new in C++, have a lifetime determined by manual memory management. They exist until explicitly deallocated using delete. Dynamic variables are stored on the heap.

```cpp
int* dynamicVar = new int; // Dynamic
lifetime
// Use dynamicVar
delete dynamicVar; // Release the memory
when done
```

Variable Shadowing

Variable shadowing occurs when a variable declared in an inner scope has the same name as a variable in an outer scope. In such cases, the inner variable "shadows" the outer one, making the outer variable temporarily inaccessible within the inner scope.

```cpp
int x = 10;

void myFunction() {
    int x = 5; // Inner variable x shadows
the outer one
    // Access the inner x
}

// Access the outer x
```

Inside myFunction, the inner variable x takes precedence over the outer variable with the same name. To access the outer variable, you can use scope resolution with the :: operator:

```
int x = 10;

void myFunction() {
    int x = 5; // Inner variable x shadows
the outer one
    ::x = 15;  // Access the outer x using
scope resolution
}
```

Understanding the scope and lifetime of variables is crucial for writing correct and efficient C++ programs. It helps you manage memory effectively and ensures that variables are accessible where needed within your code.

## 5.6 Recursion

Recursion is a powerful programming technique where a function calls itself to solve a problem. It's particularly useful for solving problems that can be broken down into smaller, similar subproblems. Recursive functions provide an elegant and concise way to solve complex tasks by dividing them into simpler instances.

**The Structure of Recursive Functions**

A recursive function consists of two essential parts:

1.  **Base Case(s):** A base case is a condition or set of conditions that define when the recursion should stop. When the base case is met, the recursive function stops calling itself and returns a result. It prevents the function from running indefinitely.
2.  **Recursive Case(s):** In the recursive case, the function calls itself with modified arguments. These modified arguments

bring the problem closer to the base case, gradually reducing the complexity of the problem with each recursive call.

## Example: Factorial Calculation

One classic example of a recursive function is calculating the factorial of a non-negative integer n. The factorial of n (denoted as n!) is the product of all positive integers from 1 to n. Mathematically, n! = 1 * 2 * 3 * ... * n.

```cpp
int factorial(int n) {
    // Base case: If n is 0 or 1, the
factorial is 1.
    if (n <= 1) {
        return 1;
    }

    // Recursive case: Multiply n by the
factorial of (n-1).
    return n * factorial(n - 1);
}
```

In this recursive function, the base case is when n is less than or equal to 1. In this case, the function returns 1. Otherwise, it multiplies n by the result of calling itself with n - 1. This process continues until the base case is reached.

## Example: Fibonacci Sequence

Another classic example of recursion is generating the Fibonacci sequence. The Fibonacci sequence is a series of numbers where each number is the sum of the two preceding ones, usually starting with 0 and 1.

```cpp
int fibonacci(int n) {
    // Base cases: The first two Fibonacci
numbers are 0 and 1.
    if (n == 0) {
        return 0;
```

```
} else if (n == 1) {
    return 1;
}


// Recursive case: The nth Fibonacci
number is the sum of the (n-1)th and (n-2)th
Fibonacci numbers.
    return fibonacci(n - 1) + fibonacci(n -
2);
}
```

In this recursive function, the base cases are when n is 0 or 1, in which case the function returns 0 or 1, respectively. In the recursive case, it calculates the nth Fibonacci number by summing the (n-1)th and (n-2)th Fibonacci numbers.

Pros and Cons of Recursion

**Pros of Recursion:**

- Allows for elegant and concise solutions to complex problems.
- Simplifies code by breaking problems into smaller, manageable parts.
- Can closely model problems with recursive structures.

**Cons of Recursion:**

- Recursive calls consume memory for each function call, which can lead to stack overflow errors for large inputs.
- Recursive solutions can sometimes be less efficient than iterative solutions for certain problems.
- Requires careful handling of base cases and termination conditions to avoid infinite recursion.

Recursion is a valuable tool in your programming toolkit, especially for solving problems that exhibit recursive patterns. It can make code more readable and maintainable when used appropriately. However, it's important to be mindful of base cases and potential performance issues when working with recursion.

# 6: ARRAYS AND STRINGS

## 6.1 Arrays in C++

Arrays are one of the fundamental data structures in C++, allowing you to store and manipulate collections of elements of the same data type. They provide a structured and efficient way to work with multiple values of the same kind, such as integers, floating-point numbers, or characters.

**Declaring and Initializing Arrays**

To declare an array in C++, you specify the data type of its elements, followed by the array name and the size of the array enclosed in square brackets. Here's the basic syntax:

```
data_type array_name[array_size];
```

- data_type: The type of data that the array will store (e.g., int, double, char).
- array_name: The name of the array, which you can choose.
- array_size: The number of elements the array can hold. It must be a non-negative integer.

Here's an example of declaring and initializing an integer array:

```
int numbers[5]; // Declares an integer array
of size 5
```

You can also initialize the array elements at the time of declaration:

```
int numbers[5] = {1, 2, 3, 4, 5}; //
Initializes an integer array with values
```

## Accessing Array Elements

Array elements are accessed using their index, which is a zero-based integer representing the position of the element in the array. To access an element, you use the array name followed by square brackets containing the index:

```
int thirdNumber = numbers[2]; // Accesses
the third element (index 2) of the 'numbers'
array
```

## Iterating Through Arrays

You can use loops, such as for or while, to iterate through the elements of an array. Here's an example of using a for loop to print all elements of an integer array:

```
for (int i = 0; i < 5; i++) {
    cout << numbers[i] << " ";
}
```

This loop iterates from 0 to 4, accessing each element of the numbers array.

## Common Array Operations

Arrays support various operations, including:

- Assigning values to elements.
- Modifying elements.
- Finding the size of the array.
- Sorting elements.
- Searching for specific values.

### Array Limitations

It's essential to be aware of some limitations of arrays:

1. **Fixed Size:** Arrays have a fixed size determined at compile-time. Once defined, their size cannot be changed dynamically.
2. **Sequential Access:** Elements in an array are stored sequentially in memory. This means that inserting or deleting elements in the middle of an array can be inefficient.
3. **No Built-in Bounds Checking:** C++ arrays do not perform bounds checking by default. Accessing an element outside the array's bounds can lead to undefined behavior.

To overcome these limitations, C++ provides the Standard Library container std::vector and other data structures for dynamic arrays and more advanced operations.

## 6.2 Working with Arrays

Arrays are versatile data structures in C++, offering a wide range of operations for storing, manipulating, and accessing data.

### Accessing Array Elements

Accessing individual elements of an array is crucial for data manipulation. Elements in an array are accessed using their index, which represents their position within the array. Remember that array indices in C++ are zero-based, meaning the first element is at index 0, the second at index 1, and so on.

Here's an example of accessing elements in an integer array:

```
int numbers[5] = {10, 20, 30, 40, 50};

int firstElement = numbers[0];   // Accesses
the first element (index 0)
int thirdElement = numbers[2];   // Accesses
the third element (index 2)
```

```
int lastElement = numbers[4];    // Accesses
the last element (index 4)
```

## Modifying Array Elements

You can modify the values of array elements by assigning new values to them using the assignment operator (=). For example:

```
int numbers[5] = {10, 20, 30, 40, 50};
```

```
numbers[2] = 35; // Modifies the third
element to have the value 35
numbers[4] = numbers[0] + numbers[1]; //
Computes a new value for the last element
```

## Finding the Size of an Array

In C++, you can find the size (number of elements) of an array using the sizeof operator. The sizeof operator returns the size of an object in bytes. To find the number of elements in an array, divide the size of the array by the size of one element. Here's an example:

```
int numbers[5] = {10, 20, 30, 40, 50};
int sizeOfArray = sizeof(numbers) /
sizeof(numbers[0]);
```

The variable sizeOfArray will hold the value 5, which is the size of the numbers array.

## Sorting Arrays

C++ provides various algorithms for sorting arrays. One commonly used sorting algorithm is the std::sort function from the Standard Library's <algorithm> header. Here's how you can use it to sort an integer array in ascending order:

```
#include <iostream>
#include <algorithm>
```

```
int main() {
    int numbers[5] = {40, 10, 30, 20, 50};

    std::sort(numbers, numbers + 5); //
Sorts the array in ascending order

    for (int i = 0; i < 5; i++) {
        std::cout << numbers[i] << " ";
    }

    return 0;
}
```

After sorting, the elements in the numbers array will be {10, 20, 30, 40, 50}.

**Searching Arrays**

You can search for specific values within an array using various methods. A common approach is to use a loop to iterate through the array and check each element until you find the desired value. Here's an example of searching for a specific value in an integer array:

```
int numbers[5] = {10, 20, 30, 40, 50};
int target = 30;

bool found = false;

for (int i = 0; i < 5; i++) {
    if (numbers[i] == target) {
        found = true;
        break; // Exit the loop early since
the value is found
    }
}
```

After this loop, the found variable will be true if target was found in the array.

These are some of the fundamental operations you can perform when working with arrays in C++.

# 6.3 Character Arrays and Strings

Character arrays and strings are essential for working with textual data in C++.

**Character Arrays (C-Style Strings)**

A character array, often referred to as a C-style string, is an array of characters terminated by a null character ('\0'). C-style strings are widely used for handling text data in C++.

*Declaring and Initializing Character Arrays*

To declare a character array, you specify the data type as char and provide the array name. Here's an example of declaring and initializing a character array:

```
char greeting[6] = {'H', 'e', 'l', 'l', 'o',
'\0'};
```

In this example, we declare a character array greeting to store the string "Hello," including the null character at the end.

*String Literals*

C++ allows you to declare character arrays more concisely using string literals:

```
char greeting[] = "Hello"; // Automatically
includes the null character
```

In this declaration, C++ infers the size of the array based on the length of the string literal.

*Accessing and Manipulating Character Arrays*

You can access individual characters in a character array just like any other array. For example:

```cpp
char firstChar = greeting[0]; // Accesses
the first character ('H')
```

To manipulate character arrays, you can use standard library functions from the <cstring> header, such as strcpy, strcat, and strlen. Here's an example of concatenating two character arrays:

```cpp
#include <iostream>
#include <cstring>

int main() {
    char firstName[] = "John";
    char lastName[] = "Doe";
    char fullName[20]; // Create an empty
character array to hold the full name

    strcpy(fullName, firstName); // Copy the
first name
    strcat(fullName, " ");         //
Concatenate a space
    strcat(fullName, lastName);   //
Concatenate the last name

    std::cout << "Full Name: " << fullName
<< std::endl;

    return 0;
}
```

std::string **Class**

While C-style strings are useful, C++ provides the std::string class, which offers more flexibility and convenience for working with strings.

*Declaring and Initializing* `std::string`

To declare and initialize a std::string, you simply assign it a string literal or another std::string:

```
#include <iostream>
#include <string>

int main() {
    std::string greeting = "Hello, C++";
    std::string firstName = "John";
    std::string lastName = "Doe";
    std::string fullName = firstName + " " +
lastName;

    std::cout << greeting << std::endl;
    std::cout << "Full Name: " << fullName
<< std::endl;

    return 0;
}
```

The + operator for std::string performs string concatenation.

`std::string` *Methods*

std::string provides numerous member functions for string manipulation, such as length(), substr(), find(), replace(), and more. These methods simplify common string operations and make your code more readable.

```
#include <iostream>
```

```
#include <string>

int main() {
    std::string text = "C++ programming is
fun";
    int length = text.length();
    std::string sub = text.substr(0, 3); //
Get the first 3 characters
    int index = text.find("programming"); //
Find the position of "programming"

    std::cout << "Length: " << length <<
std::endl;
    std::cout << "Substring: " << sub <<
std::endl;
    std::cout << "Index of 'programming': "
<< index << std::endl;

    return 0;
}
```

Using std::string simplifies many string-related tasks and reduces the risk of buffer overflows and memory issues associated with C-style strings.

## 6.4 String Manipulation

String manipulation is a crucial aspect of programming, especially when dealing with textual data. In C++, you have various tools and techniques to manipulate strings efficiently, whether you're working with character arrays (C-style strings) or the more versatile std::string class.

### Concatenating Strings

String concatenation is the process of combining two or more strings into a single string. In C++, you can concatenate strings using the +

operator for std::string objects or by using functions like strcat for C-style strings.

*Using std::string*

```cpp
#include <iostream>
#include <string>

int main() {
    std::string firstName = "John";
    std::string lastName = "Doe";

    std::string fullName = firstName + " " +
lastName;

    std::cout << "Full Name: " << fullName
<< std::endl;

    return 0;
}
```

*Using C-Style Strings*

```cpp
#include <iostream>
#include <cstring>

int main() {
    char firstName[] = "John";
    char lastName[] = "Doe";
    char fullName[20]; // Ensure enough
space

    strcpy(fullName, firstName);
    strcat(fullName, " ");
    strcat(fullName, lastName);

    std::cout << "Full Name: " << fullName
<< std::endl;
```

```cpp
    return 0;
}
```

## Finding and Replacing Substrings

You can find and replace substrings within a string using various methods and functions provided by C++.

*Using std::string*

```cpp
#include <iostream>
#include <string>

int main() {
    std::string text = "C++ programming is fun";

    // Find a substring
    size_t found = text.find("programming");
    if (found != std::string::npos) {
        std::cout << "Substring found at position: " << found << std::endl;
    }

    // Replace a substring
    text.replace(found, 11, "coding");

    std::cout << "Modified string: " << text << std::endl;

    return 0;
}
```

*Using C-Style Strings*

```cpp
#include <iostream>
#include <cstring>

int main() {
    char text[] = "C++ programming is fun";
```

```
    char* found = strstr(text,
"programming");

    if (found != nullptr) {
        size_t position = found - text;
        std::cout << "Substring found at
position: " << position << std::endl;

        // Replace a substring
        strncpy(found, "coding", 6);

        std::cout << "Modified string: " <<
text << std::endl;
    }

    return 0;
}
```

**Converting Between** std::string **and C-Style Strings**

You can convert between std::string and C-style strings using functions like c_str() and constructors.

*std::string to C-Style String*

```
#include <iostream>
#include <string>

int main() {
    std::string str = "Hello, C++";
    const char* cstr = str.c_str();

    std::cout << "C-Style String: " << cstr
<< std::endl;

    return 0;
}
```

*C-Style String to std::string*

```cpp
#include <iostream>
#include <string>

int main() {
    const char* cstr = "Hello, C++";
    std::string str(cstr);

    std::cout << "std::string: " << str <<
std::endl;

    return 0;
}
```

**String Manipulation Functions**

C++ provides various functions and methods for string manipulation in addition to those mentioned earlier. These include length() to find the length of a string, substr() to extract a substring, and many others. Familiarizing yourself with these functions will greatly enhance your ability to work with strings effectively.

String manipulation is a critical skill when working with textual data in C++. Whether you're building search algorithms, parsing text files, or simply formatting output, mastering string manipulation techniques is essential for writing robust and versatile programs.

# 7: POINTERS AND REFERENCES

## 7.1 Introduction to Pointers

Pointers are a fundamental concept in C++ and a key feature that sets C++ apart from many other programming languages. At their core, pointers are variables that store memory addresses. They provide a way to access and manipulate data directly in memory, offering a level of control and efficiency that can be extremely useful in a wide range of programming scenarios.

### Understanding Memory Addresses

In a computer's memory, every byte of data has a unique address. Think of memory as a vast array of boxes, each with a specific address. When you declare a variable in C++, it occupies a particular location in memory, and you can think of that variable as residing in one of these boxes.

A pointer, instead of holding the data itself, holds the memory address of the data. It's like having a piece of paper with the box's address instead of the actual contents of the box. Pointers allow you to locate and interact with data in memory.

### Declaring Pointers

To declare a pointer in C++, you use the * symbol followed by the data type of the variable it will point to. Here's the basic syntax:

```
data_type* pointer_name;
```

- data_type: The data type of the variable that the pointer will point to (e.g., int, double, char).
- pointer_name: The name you give to the pointer variable.

For example, to declare a pointer to an integer variable:

```
int* ptr;
```

### Initializing Pointers

It's essential to initialize pointers before using them to ensure they point to valid memory addresses. Uninitialized pointers, often called "wild pointers," can lead to undefined behavior and crashes.

Pointers can be initialized in several ways:

1. **Null Pointer:** A pointer can be initialized to nullptr, indicating that it doesn't currently point to any valid memory location.

```
int* ptr = nullptr;
```

2. **Address of a Variable:** You can initialize a pointer with the address of an existing variable.

```
int num = 42;
int* ptr = &num; // 'ptr' now points to
the 'num' variable
```

### Dereferencing Pointers

Dereferencing a pointer means accessing the value it points to. You use the * operator to dereference a pointer. For example:

```
int num = 42;
int* ptr = &num; // 'ptr' points to 'num'
```

```
int value = *ptr; // Dereferencing 'ptr' to
access the value (value will be 42)
```

In this code, *ptr retrieves the value stored at the memory address pointed to by ptr, which is 42.

**Pointers and Memory Management**

Pointers are invaluable for dynamic memory allocation and deallocation. Functions like new and delete enable you to allocate memory on the heap and control its lifespan using pointers.

# 7.2 Pointers and Memory Management

Pointers play a vital role in managing memory in C++. They provide the ability to allocate and deallocate memory dynamically, which can be especially useful when working with data structures of varying sizes or lifetimes.

**Dynamic Memory Allocation with** new

C++ provides the new operator to allocate memory dynamically on the heap. Dynamic memory allocation allows you to create objects with a lifetime that extends beyond the scope in which they were created. This is in contrast to automatic storage duration, where variables are created on the stack and have a limited scope.

Here's how you can use new to allocate memory for a single integer:

```
int* dynamicInt = new int; // Allocate
memory for an integer on the heap
*dynamicInt = 42; // Store the value 42 in
the dynamically allocated memory
```

In this example, dynamicInt is a pointer to an integer allocated on the heap. The *dynamicInt notation is used to access and modify the value stored at that memory location.

## Dynamic Memory Deallocation with delete

Allocated memory should be properly deallocated to prevent memory leaks. The delete operator is used to release memory that was previously allocated with new. Failing to deallocate memory can lead to memory leaks, where the program consumes more and more memory over time.

Here's how you can deallocate the previously allocated memory for the integer:

```cpp
delete dynamicInt; // Deallocate the memory
pointed to by 'dynamicInt'
```

After using delete, it's a good practice to set the pointer to nullptr to avoid potential issues:

```cpp
dynamicInt = nullptr; // Reset the pointer
to nullptr
```

## Dynamic Arrays

You can also use new to allocate arrays dynamically. When allocating arrays, you specify the number of elements in square brackets:

```cpp
cpp
int* dynamicArray = new int[5]; // Allocate
an array of 5 integers on the heap

// Initialize elements of the dynamic array
for (int i = 0; i < 5; i++) {
    dynamicArray[i] = i * 10;
}
```

Don't forget to deallocate dynamic arrays with delete[]:

```cpp
delete[] dynamicArray; // Deallocate the
dynamic array
```

```
dynamicArray = nullptr; // Reset the pointer
to nullptr
```

**Avoiding Memory Leaks**

To ensure your program doesn't leak memory, always pair each new operation with a corresponding delete operation. If you lose all references to dynamically allocated memory without deallocating it, you create a memory leak.

Using modern C++ practices, you can avoid manual memory management altogether by using smart pointers such as std::unique_ptr and std::shared_ptr. These smart pointers automatically manage memory for you, releasing it when it's no longer needed.

# 7.3 References

References in C++ provide a convenient way to create aliases or alternative names for existing variables. They allow you to work with variables indirectly without the need for pointers and provide an elegant solution for passing arguments to functions by reference.

**Declaring References**

A reference is declared by using the & symbol following the data type. Here's the basic syntax:

```
data_type& reference_name =
existing_variable;
```

- data_type: The data type of the variable to which the reference refers (e.g., int, double, char).
- reference_name: The name you give to the reference.

For example, to declare a reference to an integer variable:

```
int num = 42;
```

```
int& refNum = num; // 'refNum' is a
reference to 'num'
```

In this example, refNum is an alias for the num variable.

## Working with References

References can be used just like regular variables. When you modify the reference, you are modifying the original variable it refers to. Consider this example:

```
int num = 42;
int& refNum = num; // 'refNum' is a
reference to 'num'

refNum = 99; // Modifies 'num' indirectly
through 'refNum'
```

After this code executes, the value of num becomes 99.

## References as Function Parameters

One of the most common uses of references is passing variables to functions by reference. This allows functions to modify the original variables directly rather than working with copies.

```
void incrementByReference(int& value) {
    value++; // Modifies the original
variable
}

int main() {
    int num = 42;
    incrementByReference(num);

    // 'num' is now 43

    return 0;
}
```

By passing num by reference to the incrementByReference function, we can modify the value of num within the function.

**Constant References**

You can declare references as const, which means the referenced variable cannot be modified through the reference. This is useful when you want to pass variables to functions without allowing those functions to change the original values.

```cpp
void printValue(const int& value) {
    // value++; // Error! Cannot modify
'value' since it's a const reference
    std::cout << "Value: " << value <<
std::endl;
}

int main() {
    int num = 42;
    printValue(num);

    // 'num' remains 42

    return 0;
}
```

**Reference Variables**

Reference variables are references to other references. While they may not be used as frequently as references to variables, they have their uses in specific scenarios.

```cpp
int num = 42;
int& refNum = num; // Reference to 'num'
int& refToRefNum = refNum; // Reference to
'refNum'
```

Keep in mind that using reference variables can make your code more complex, so use them judiciously.

References are a valuable tool in C++ for creating efficient and clean code. They provide a means of working with variables indirectly while avoiding the complexities of pointers. When used correctly, references can make your code more readable and maintainable, especially when passing arguments to functions or modifying variables in various parts of your program.

# 7.4 Pointers vs. References

Pointers and references are both powerful tools in C++ for working with memory and data. They serve similar purposes, allowing you to access and manipulate variables indirectly, but they have distinct differences and use cases.

### Declaration and Initialization

**Pointers:**

- Declared using the * symbol, e.g., int* ptr.
- Must be explicitly initialized with a memory address or set to nullptr.
- Can be reassigned to point to different memory locations.

```
int num = 42;
int* ptr = &num; // 'ptr' points to 'num'
ptr = nullptr;   // 'ptr' no longer points
to any valid memory
```

**References:**

- Declared using the & symbol, e.g., int& ref.
- Must be initialized when declared, and they cannot be reassigned to refer to a different variable.
- Provide an alias for an existing variable.

```
int num = 42;
int& ref = num; // 'ref' is an alias for
'num'
```

## Null Values

### Pointers:

- Can hold a special null value represented by nullptr, indicating that they do not point to any valid memory location.
- Useful when a pointer may not always have a valid target.

```
int* ptr = nullptr; // 'ptr' does not point
to valid memory
```

### References:

- Cannot hold a null value.
- Must always refer to an existing variable.
- Attempts to create a reference without an initial value result in a compile-time error.

```
int& ref; // Error: references must be
initialized
```

## Memory Management

### Pointers:

- Often used for dynamic memory allocation and deallocation using new and delete.
- Provide fine-grained control over memory, but with the responsibility of manual memory management.

```
int* dynamicInt = new int; // Allocate
memory
*dynamicInt = 42;          // Use allocated
memory
delete dynamicInt;         // Deallocate
memory
```

## References:

- Do not allocate or deallocate memory; they are purely aliases for existing variables.
- Safer in terms of memory management as they don't introduce memory leaks.

```
int num = 42;
int& refNum = num; // 'refNum' is an alias
for 'num', no dynamic memory involved
```

## Use Cases

## Pointers:

- Suitable for situations where you need dynamic memory allocation or manipulation of memory addresses.
- Commonly used for building data structures like linked lists, trees, and dynamic arrays.
- Useful when working with functions that return memory addresses or need to accept variable-length arrays.

## References:

- Ideal for passing arguments to functions when you want to modify the original data.
- Provide a clean and readable way to work with existing variables without introducing memory management complexities.
- Useful when you don't need to change what the reference refers to, but rather how you interact with it.

## Guidelines for Choosing

- Use references when you want to work with existing variables directly and pass them to functions by reference for modification.

- Use pointers when you need dynamic memory allocation, want to work with memory addresses directly, or require reassigning to different memory locations.
- Use references for readability and safety in many scenarios, but choose pointers when fine-grained control over memory is necessary.

The choice between pointers and references ultimately depends on the specific requirements of your program and the level of control and flexibility you need when dealing with memory and data.

## 7.5 Dynamic Memory Allocation

Dynamic memory allocation is a powerful feature in C++ that allows you to allocate memory during program execution rather than at compile time. This flexibility is especially valuable when dealing with data structures of variable sizes or lifetimes.

### The new Operator

In C++, the new operator is used to allocate memory dynamically on the heap. When you use new, it requests a block of memory from the system and returns a pointer to the first byte of that block. You can use this pointer to work with the allocated memory.

Here's the basic syntax for using new to allocate memory for a single variable:

```
data_type* pointer_name = new data_type;
```

- data_type: The data type of the variable you want to allocate (e.g., int, double, struct).
- pointer_name: The name you give to the pointer that will hold the address of the allocated memory.

For example, to allocate memory for an integer:

```
int* dynamicInt = new int; // Allocate
memory for an integer on the heap
*dynamicInt = 42; // Store the value 42 in
the dynamically allocated memory
```

## Dynamic Arrays

You can also use new to allocate arrays dynamically. When allocating arrays, you specify the number of elements in square brackets:

```
data_type* array_pointer_name = new
data_type[size];
```

- data_type: The data type of the array elements.
- array_pointer_name: The name you give to the pointer that will hold the address of the allocated array.
- size: The number of elements in the array.

For example, to allocate an array of 5 integers:

```
int* dynamicArray = new int[5]; // Allocate
an array of 5 integers on the heap

// Initialize elements of the dynamic array
for (int i = 0; i < 5; i++) {
    dynamicArray[i] = i * 10;
}
```

## The delete Operator

Allocated memory should be properly deallocated to prevent memory leaks. The delete operator is used to release memory that was previously allocated with new. Failing to deallocate memory can lead to memory leaks, where the program consumes more and more memory over time.

Here's how you can use delete to deallocate memory for a single variable:

```
delete pointer_name; // Deallocate the
memory pointed to by 'pointer_name'
```

And for deallocating a dynamically allocated array:

```
delete[] array_pointer_name; // Deallocate
the dynamic array
```

After using delete, it's a good practice to set the pointer to nullptr to avoid potential issues:

```
pointer_name = nullptr; // Reset the pointer
to nullptr
```

**Smart Pointers**

While manual memory management with new and delete is powerful, it can be error-prone. C++ provides smart pointers like std::unique_ptr and std::shared_ptr that automatically manage memory for you. Smart pointers ensure timely deallocation and help prevent common memory-related issues such as double deletion.

```
#include <memory>

std::unique_ptr<int> smartInt =
std::make_unique<int>(42); // Smart pointer
for an integer

std::shared_ptr<int> sharedInt =
std::make_shared<int>(42); // Shared smart
pointer for an integer
```

Smart pointers are especially useful when dealing with complex data structures and managing resources.

Dynamic memory allocation with pointers provides you with the flexibility to create and manage memory at runtime. However, it also comes with the responsibility of proper memory deallocation to avoid memory leaks. Smart pointers offer a safer and more convenient alternative for many scenarios, making memory management in C++ more manageable and less error-prone.

# 8: OBJECT-ORIENTED PROGRAMMING

## 8.1 Classes and Objects

In the world of Object-Oriented Programming (OOP), classes and objects are the foundation upon which you build your code. Classes serve as blueprints or templates for creating objects, and objects are instances of those classes. Understanding classes and objects is crucial to embracing the OOP paradigm in C++.

**Classes: Blueprints for Objects**

A class is a user-defined data type that represents a concept, entity, or object in your program. It serves as a blueprint that defines the properties (data members) and behaviors (member functions) that objects of that class will have. These properties and behaviors are encapsulated within the class, making it a self-contained unit.

Here's a basic syntax for defining a class in C++:

```
class ClassName {
public:
    // Data members (attributes)
    data_type member_variable1;
    data_type member_variable2;

    // Member functions (methods)
    return_type
member_function1(parameters);
    return_type
member_function2(parameters);
```

};

- ClassName: The name you give to the class.
- data_type: The data type of the member variables.
- member_variable1, member_variable2: Properties or attributes of the class.
- return_type: The data type of the value returned by member functions.
- member_function1, member_function2: Methods or behaviors of the class.
- parameters: Any input values that the member functions accept.

For example, here's a simple class Person:

```cpp
class Person {
public:
    // Data members
    std::string name;
    int age;

    // Member function to display
information
    void displayInfo() {
        std::cout << "Name: " << name << ",
Age: " << age << std::endl;
    }
};
```

**Objects: Instances of Classes**

An object is an instance of a class, created based on the blueprint defined by the class. When you create an object, you allocate memory for its data members, effectively instantiating the class. Each object has its own set of data members and can invoke the member functions defined in its class.

Here's how you create an object from a class:

```
ClassName objectName; // Create an object of
the class
```

For our Person class:

```
Person person1; // Create a 'Person' object
```

**Accessing Members of Objects**

Once you have an object, you can access its data members and invoke its member functions using the dot . operator:

```
objectName.member_variable1 = value; //
Access and modify a data member
objectName.member_function1(arguments); //
Invoke a member function
```

For our Person object:

```
person1.name = "Alice"; // Access and set
the 'name' data member
person1.age = 30; // Access and set the
'age' data member
person1.displayInfo(); // Invoke the
'displayInfo' member function
```

**The Constructor and Destructor**

Classes can have special member functions called constructors and destructors. A constructor is used to initialize the object when it's created, while a destructor is used to clean up resources when the object is destroyed.

```
class ClassName {
public:
    ClassName() {
        // Constructor code here
    }
```

```
    ~ClassName() {
        // Destructor code here
    }
};
```

Constructors have the same name as the class and do not have a return type. Destructors have the same name as the class with a tilde (~) preceding it and also do not have a return type.

# 8.2 Constructors and Destructors

Constructors and destructors are special member functions in C++ classes that play a crucial role in object initialization and cleanup. Constructors are used to initialize the state of objects when they are created, while destructors are responsible for releasing resources and performing cleanup when objects go out of scope or are explicitly destroyed.

**Constructors: Initializing Objects**

Constructors are invoked automatically when an object is created. They allow you to initialize the object's data members, ensuring that the object starts in a valid state. You can define one or more constructors for a class, each with a specific set of parameters or behaviors.

*Default Constructor*

A default constructor is a constructor with no parameters. If you don't define any constructors for a class, C++ provides a default constructor automatically. It initializes data members to default values (e.g., zero for numeric types, empty for strings).

```
class MyClass {
public:
    // Default constructor
    MyClass() {
```

```
        // Initialization code here
    }
};
```

*Parameterized Constructors*

Parameterized constructors accept one or more parameters, allowing you to initialize data members based on provided values during object creation.

```
class MyClass {
public:
    // Parameterized constructor
    MyClass(int value) {
        // Initialization code here using
'value'
    }
};
```

*Overloaded Constructors*

You can define multiple constructors with different parameter lists, which is known as constructor overloading. This allows you to create objects in various ways, depending on the parameters provided.

```
class MyClass {
public:
    // Default constructor
    MyClass() {
        // Initialization code for default
constructor
    }

    // Parameterized constructor
    MyClass(int value) {
        // Initialization code using 'value'
    }

    // Another parameterized constructor
```

```
    MyClass(int value1, int value2) {
        // Initialization code using
'value1' and 'value2'
    }
};
```

## Destructors: Cleanup and Resource Release

Destructors are used to clean up resources, release memory, and perform any necessary cleanup tasks when an object goes out of scope or is explicitly destroyed. A class can have only one destructor, and it has the same name as the class, preceded by a tilde ($\sim$).

```
class MyClass {
public:
    // Destructor
    ~MyClass() {
        // Cleanup code here
    }
};
```

Destructors are crucial when a class allocates resources such as dynamic memory, files, or network connections during its lifetime. They ensure that these resources are properly released, preventing resource leaks.

## Implicit vs. Explicit Object Creation

When you create an object, the appropriate constructor is invoked automatically based on the object creation syntax. For example:

```
MyClass object1; // Calls the default
constructor
MyClass object2(42); // Calls the
parameterized constructor with '42'
```

Additionally, when an object goes out of scope or is explicitly destroyed, the destructor is called automatically:

```
{
    MyClass object3; // Object3 is created
and the default constructor is called
} // Object3 goes out of scope, and its
destructor is called
```

Explicitly calling constructors and destructors is not common in regular C++ programming, as C++ handles these operations automatically for you.

Constructors and destructors are essential for ensuring proper object initialization and cleanup. They allow you to manage the lifetime and resources associated with objects, making your C++ code more robust and reliable.

# 8.3 Member Functions

Member functions are an integral part of classes in C++. They define the behavior and operations that objects of a class can perform. These functions encapsulate the logic related to the class and provide a way for objects to interact with and manipulate their data members.

**Defining Member Functions**

Member functions are defined within the class declaration and are associated with objects of that class. They are declared and implemented just like regular functions but are prefixed with the class name followed by the scope resolution operator ::. Here's the syntax for defining member functions:

```
class ClassName {
public:
    // Member function declaration
    return_type memberFunction(parameters) {
        // Function implementation here
    }
};
```

- ClassName: The name of the class to which the member function belongs.
- return_type: The data type of the value returned by the member function.
- memberFunction: The name of the member function.
- parameters: Any input values that the member function accepts.

For example, here's a class Rectangle with a member function calculateArea:

```cpp
class Rectangle {
public:
    // Member function to calculate area
    double calculateArea(double length,
double width) {
        return length * width;
    }
};
```

**Invoking Member Functions**

Member functions are invoked using objects of the class. You use the dot . operator to call a member function on an object:

```cpp
objectName.memberFunction(arguments);
```

For our Rectangle class:

```cpp
Rectangle rectangleObject;
double area =
rectangleObject.calculateArea(5.0, 3.0); //
Invoking the member function
```

In this example, we create a Rectangle object and call the calculateArea member function on it, passing the length and width as arguments.

## Accessing Data Members

Member functions have access to the data members of the class, allowing them to manipulate the object's state. Data members are accessed using the same dot . operator:

```cpp
class MyClass {
public:
    int dataMember; // Data member

    // Member function to modify the data member
    void modifyData(int newValue) {
        dataMember = newValue;
    }
};

MyClass object;
object.dataMember = 42; // Accessing the data member
object.modifyData(99); // Invoking the member function to modify the data member
```

## Member Functions and Encapsulation

Member functions play a critical role in achieving encapsulation, one of the core principles of Object-Oriented Programming. Encapsulation involves bundling data and the methods that operate on that data within a single unit (the class). This concept allows you to hide the internal details of an object while providing a well-defined interface for interacting with it.

By encapsulating data and behavior within classes and providing member functions to manipulate that data, you create a clear and controlled way to work with objects. This promotes code organization, reusability, and maintainability.

Types of Member Functions

In addition to regular member functions, C++ supports other types of member functions, including:

- **Static Member Functions:** These functions are associated with the class itself rather than with individual objects. They can be called using the class name and do not require an object.
- **Const Member Functions:** Declaring a member function as const indicates that it does not modify the object's state. Const member functions can be called on const objects, providing a guarantee of non-modification.
- **Operator Overloading:** You can overload operators using member functions, allowing objects to work with operators such as +, -, *, and == as if they were built-in types.

Member functions are the heart of classes in C++. They define how objects interact with and manipulate their data, enabling you to model real-world entities in a structured and organized manner.

# 8.4 Access Control (Public, Private, Protected)

Access control is a fundamental concept in C++ that allows you to control the visibility and accessibility of class members, including data members and member functions. By specifying access levels for class members, you can enforce encapsulation, protect sensitive data, and define how objects interact with the outside world. In C++, there are three access control keywords: public, private, and protected.

Public Access

Members declared under the public access specifier are accessible from anywhere in your program, including outside the class. This means that you can access public members using objects of the class.

```
class MyClass {
public:
```

```
    int publicData; // Public data member

    void publicFunction() {
        // Public member function
    }
};
```

You can access public members like this:

```
MyClass myObject;
myObject.publicData = 42; // Accessing
public data member
myObject.publicFunction(); // Invoking
public member function
```

Public members provide an interface for interacting with objects of the class and are often used to define the essential functionalities that objects should provide to the outside world.

**Private Access**

Members declared under the private access specifier are not accessible from outside the class. They are hidden from the external world and can only be accessed by member functions within the same class.

```
class MyClass {
private:
    int privateData; // Private data member

    void privateFunction() {
        // Private member function
    }
};
```

Attempting to access private members directly from outside the class will result in a compilation error:

```
MyClass myObject;
```

```
myObject.privateData = 42; // Error:
'privateData' is private
myObject.privateFunction(); // Error:
'privateFunction' is private
```

Private members are used to encapsulate the internal details of a class, protecting them from external interference. This is a fundamental principle of object-oriented programming known as encapsulation.

**Protected Access**

Members declared under the protected access specifier are similar to private members in that they are not accessible from outside the class. However, they have an important role in class inheritance, as they are inherited by derived classes.

```
class MyBaseClass {
protected:
    int protectedData; // Protected data
member
};
```

Derived classes can access protected members of their base class:

```
class MyDerivedClass : public MyBaseClass {
public:
    void accessProtected() {
        protectedData = 42; // Accessing
protected data member
    }
};
```

Protected members provide a level of access control that allows derived classes to inherit and use the data members or functions of their base class while still restricting access from external sources.

Access Control and Encapsulation

Access control plays a crucial role in encapsulation, which is one of the key principles of Object-Oriented Programming (OOP). Encapsulation involves bundling data and methods that operate on that data within a single unit (the class) and controlling access to that unit. By defining appropriate access specifiers (public, private, protected), you can achieve the following:

- **Public Members:** Define the interface for interacting with objects from the outside world, making essential functionalities accessible.
- **Private Members:** Hide internal details and sensitive data, preventing direct external access and ensuring data integrity.
- **Protected Members:** Allow derived classes to access and inherit base class members while maintaining encapsulation.

Understanding access control is essential for designing classes that provide a well-defined and secure interface for interacting with objects. It promotes code modularity, reusability, and maintainability, which are core principles of OOP.

# 8.5 Inheritance and Polymorphism

Inheritance and polymorphism are two fundamental concepts in Object-Oriented Programming (OOP) that allow you to create hierarchies of classes, share functionality, and write more flexible and extensible code.

Inheritance

**Inheritance** is a mechanism that allows you to create a new class (called the **derived class** or **subclass**) based on an existing class (called the **base class** or **superclass**). The derived class inherits the properties and behaviors (data members and member functions) of the base class and can also extend or modify them.

*Syntax for Inheritance*

To create a derived class, you use a colon (:) followed by the access specifier (public, private, or protected) and the name of the base class:

```
class BaseClass {
public:
    // Base class members
};

class DerivedClass : public BaseClass {
public:
    // Derived class members
};
```

- BaseClass: The name of the base class.
- DerivedClass: The name of the derived class.
- public: The access specifier indicating the type of inheritance (public, private, or protected).

*Access Control in Inheritance*

- **Public Inheritance:** Public members of the base class become public members of the derived class. Protected members of the base class become protected members of the derived class. Private members of the base class are not accessible in the derived class.
- **Private Inheritance:** Public and protected members of the base class become private members of the derived class. Private members of the base class are not accessible in the derived class.
- **Protected Inheritance:** Public and protected members of the base class become protected members of the derived class. Private members of the base class are not accessible in the derived class.

*Example of Inheritance*

```cpp
class Animal {
public:
    void eat() {
        std::cout << "Animal is eating." <<
std::endl;
    }
};

class Dog : public Animal {
public:
    void bark() {
        std::cout << "Dog is barking." <<
std::endl;
    }
};
```

In this example, the Dog class inherits the eat function from the Animal class. The Dog class also has its own member function, bark.

## Polymorphism

**Polymorphism** is the ability of different objects to respond to the same message (method call) in their unique ways. In C++, polymorphism is achieved through virtual functions and inheritance.

*Virtual Functions*

A **virtual function** is a member function declared in a base class with the virtual keyword and can be overridden by derived classes. Virtual functions allow dynamic binding of functions at runtime, enabling you to call the appropriate function for a specific object.

```cpp
class Shape {
public:
    virtual void draw() {
```

```cpp
        std::cout << "Drawing a shape." <<
std::endl;
    }
};

class Circle : public Shape {
public:
    void draw() override {
        std::cout << "Drawing a circle." <<
std::endl;
    }
};

class Square : public Shape {
public:
    void draw() override {
        std::cout << "Drawing a square." <<
std::endl;
    }
};
```

In this example, the Shape class has a virtual function draw, which is overridden in the Circle and Square classes. When you call the draw function on a Shape object, the appropriate derived class function is invoked based on the object's actual type.

*Polymorphism in Action*

```cpp
Shape* shape1 = new Circle();
Shape* shape2 = new Square();

shape1->draw(); // Calls Circle's draw
shape2->draw(); // Calls Square's draw
```

In this code, even though the pointers shape1 and shape2 are of type Shape*, the actual function called depends on the type of the object they point to. This is called **runtime polymorphism** or **dynamic polymorphism**.

## Benefits of Inheritance and Polymorphism

- **Code Reusability:** Inheritance allows you to reuse existing classes, reducing code duplication.
- **Flexibility:** Polymorphism enables you to write generic code that can work with objects of different derived classes.
- **Hierarchy Modeling:** You can model real-world relationships and hierarchies of objects in a natural way.

Inheritance and polymorphism are powerful tools in object-oriented programming that help you create more organized, maintainable, and extensible code. They are fundamental concepts for building complex software systems.

# 8.6 Operator Overloading

Operator overloading is a powerful feature in C++ that allows you to define custom behaviors for operators when used with user-defined data types, such as classes. It allows you to extend the functionality of operators to work with objects of your own classes, providing a more intuitive and natural syntax.

## Basics of Operator Overloading

C++ allows you to overload a variety of operators, including arithmetic operators (+, -, *, /), comparison operators (==, !=, <, >, <=, >=), and even assignment operators (=), among others. When you overload an operator for a class, you define how objects of that class should behave when that operator is used with them.

### *Syntax for Operator Overloading*

To overload an operator for a class, you define a member function within the class, and the function name is the operator you want to overload. For binary operators (operators that take two operands), the overloaded function typically takes one parameter representing the right operand.

```cpp
class MyClass {
public:
    MyClass operator+(const MyClass& other)
{
        // Define the behavior of the +
operator for objects of MyClass
        MyClass result;
        // Perform addition here
        return result;
    }
};
```

*Example of Operator Overloading*

Let's take an example of overloading the + operator for a class representing complex numbers:

```cpp
class Complex {
public:
    double real;
    double imag;

    Complex operator+(const Complex& other)
{
        Complex result;
        result.real = this->real +
other.real;
        result.imag = this->imag +
other.imag;
        return result;
    }
};
```

With this operator overloading, you can add two Complex objects using the + operator:

```cpp
Complex num1, num2, sum;
// Initialize num1 and num2
```

```
sum = num1 + num2; // Calls the overloaded +
operator
```

## Rules for Operator Overloading

When overloading operators, there are some rules and guidelines to follow:

1. **Operator Overloading Functions:** Overloaded operator functions should be member functions of a class or defined as global functions with at least one operand of user-defined type.
2. **Return Type:** For most operators, the return type should match the type of the object for which the operator is overloaded.
3. **Parameter(s):** For binary operators, the right operand should typically be passed as a parameter.
4. **Operator Syntax:** You cannot change the syntax or the precedence of an operator when overloading it.
5. **Operator Limitations:** Some operators, such as . (member access), :: (scope resolution), ?: (ternary conditional), and sizeof, cannot be overloaded.

## Commonly Overloaded Operators

In addition to the arithmetic and comparison operators, other operators like << and >> (stream insertion and extraction), = (assignment), [] (subscripting), and () (function call) are often overloaded for specific class types to provide more intuitive functionality.

## Example: Overloading the << Operator for Output

```cpp
class MyClass {
public:
    int data;
    MyClass(int val) : data(val) {}
```

```
    friend std::ostream&
operator<<(std::ostream& os, const MyClass&
obj) {
        os << obj.data;
        return os;
    }
};
```

With this operator overloading, you can easily output objects of MyClass using cout:

```
MyClass obj(42);
std::cout << obj << std::endl; // Prints: 42
```

Operator overloading can make your classes more expressive and user-friendly, allowing you to work with objects in a way that's natural and intuitive for your application's domain. However, it should be used judiciously and consistently to avoid confusion and maintain code readability.

# 8.7 Object-Oriented Design Principles

Object-Oriented Programming (OOP) is not just about writing code; it's also about designing software in a way that promotes modularity, reusability, and maintainability. To achieve these goals, software developers often follow a set of design principles that guide the creation of classes and objects.

**1.** Single Responsibility Principle (SRP)

The SRP states that a class should have only one reason to change, meaning it should have only one responsibility or job. When designing classes, it's important to keep them focused on a specific task. If a class becomes too complex with multiple responsibilities, it becomes harder to maintain and extend.

**2.** Open-Closed Principle (OCP)

The OCP suggests that software entities (classes, modules, functions, etc.) should be open for extension but closed for modification. This means that you should be able to add new functionality to a system without altering its existing code. You achieve this by using techniques like inheritance, interfaces, and abstract classes to allow for future extensions.

**3.** Liskov Substitution Principle (LSP)

The LSP states that objects of a derived class should be able to replace objects of the base class without affecting the correctness of the program. This principle ensures that derived classes maintain the same behavior and adhere to the same contracts as their base classes, promoting polymorphism and substitutability.

**4.** Interface Segregation Principle (ISP)

The ISP emphasizes that clients should not be forced to depend on interfaces they do not use. It encourages breaking down large, monolithic interfaces into smaller, more specific ones. This avoids the problem of clients being burdened with methods they don't need, making the system more modular and maintainable.

**5.** Dependency Inversion Principle (DIP)

The DIP promotes high-level modules not depending on low-level modules but rather both depending on abstractions (interfaces or abstract classes). This principle encourages decoupling and allows for more flexibility in choosing concrete implementations at runtime.

**6.** Composition Over Inheritance

This is a design principle that suggests favoring composition (combining objects) over inheritance (extending classes) to achieve code reuse. Composition is often more flexible and less prone to issues like the diamond problem in multiple inheritance.

## 7. Don't Repeat Yourself (DRY)

The DRY principle advises against duplicating code. Instead, code should be modularized, and common functionality should be abstracted into reusable components (e.g., functions or classes). This reduces maintenance effort and the risk of bugs due to inconsistent code.

## 8. Keep It Simple, Stupid (KISS)

KISS encourages simplicity in design. Complex solutions should be avoided unless they are truly necessary. Simple designs are often easier to understand, maintain, and extend.

## 9. Separation of Concerns (SoC)

SoC suggests breaking a software system into distinct, loosely coupled modules or components, each handling a specific concern or responsibility. This enhances maintainability and facilitates concurrent development.

## 10. Law of Demeter (LoD)

The LoD, also known as the "principle of least knowledge," states that an object should only interact with its immediate neighbors and not have extensive knowledge about the internal workings of other objects. This reduces coupling between classes and promotes encapsulation.

## Applying Design Principles

While these design principles provide valuable guidelines, their application may vary depending on the specific requirements and context of your software project. Effective object-oriented design involves a balance between these principles to create well-structured, maintainable, and extensible software systems.

By adhering to these principles, you can create object-oriented designs that are not only efficient but also robust, adaptable, and easy to maintain, resulting in software that stands the test of time and evolves gracefully as requirements change.

# 9: EXCEPTION HANDLING

## 9.1 Handling Errors and Exceptions

In the world of software development, errors and unexpected situations are inevitable. You can't always predict when a file will be missing, a network connection will fail, or a calculation will result in a division by zero. However, you can prepare your code to gracefully handle these situations using exception handling.

### What Are Exceptions?

An **exception** is an abnormal condition or event that occurs during the execution of a program and disrupts its normal flow. Exceptions can represent various scenarios, such as:

- Division by zero
- File not found
- Network errors
- Invalid input
- Out-of-memory conditions

Exceptions are a way for your program to communicate that something has gone wrong, allowing you to respond appropriately.

### The Need for Exception Handling

Without exception handling, encountering an error could lead to program termination or unpredictable behavior. Exception handling provides a structured mechanism to:

1. Detect exceptions: Your code can identify when something unexpected occurs.
2. Report exceptions: It allows you to provide information about the error, making debugging easier.
3. Handle exceptions: You can implement custom logic to deal with errors gracefully, potentially recovering from the error or taking alternative actions.

**Exception Handling in C++**

In C++, exception handling is accomplished using a combination of keywords and constructs, primarily:

- try: A block of code where exceptions might occur.
- catch: A block of code that handles exceptions.
- throw: A statement used to throw an exception.
- exception: A class hierarchy representing different types of exceptions.

Here's a basic structure of exception handling in C++:

```
try {
    // Code that may throw an exception
}
catch (ExceptionType1& e) {
    // Handle ExceptionType1
}
catch (ExceptionType2& e) {
    // Handle ExceptionType2
}
// ...
catch (...) {
    // Catch-all for other exceptions
}
```

- Inside the try block, you place the code that might throw exceptions.

- In the catch blocks, you specify the type of exception you want to handle. If an exception of that type is thrown in the try block, the corresponding catch block is executed.
- The catch (...) block is a catch-all for any unhandled exceptions.

**Example: Division by Zero**

```cpp
try {
    int dividend = 10;
    int divisor = 0;
    if (divisor == 0) {
        throw std::runtime_error("Division
by zero is not allowed.");
    }
    int result = dividend / divisor;
    std::cout << "Result: " << result <<
std::endl;
}
catch (const std::exception& e) {
    std::cerr << "Exception: " << e.what()
<< std::endl;
}
```

In this example, we try to divide dividend by divisor. If divisor is zero, we throw an exception of type std::runtime_error. The corresponding catch block then handles the exception and provides an error message.

Exception handling is a crucial aspect of writing robust and reliable code. By detecting and handling exceptions gracefully, you can improve the resilience of your programs, making them more user-friendly and easier to debug.

## 9.2 try-catch Blocks

In C++, the try and catch blocks form the foundation of exception handling. These constructs allow you to delineate the code that might throw exceptions (the try block) and specify how to handle those exceptions (the catch block or blocks).

## The try Block

The try block is where you place the code that might throw exceptions. It's a defined scope within which you anticipate potential exceptions. If an exception occurs within the try block, the control flow is transferred to the appropriate catch block.

```
try {
    // Code that may throw exceptions
}
catch (ExceptionType1& e) {
    // Handle ExceptionType1
}
// ...
```

- Inside the try block, you write the code that may result in exceptions.
- Multiple catch blocks can follow a single try block, each handling different types of exceptions. The program will jump to the first catch block that matches the thrown exception's type.

## The catch Blocks

A catch block specifies how to handle exceptions of a particular type. You can have multiple catch blocks to handle different exception types or situations.

```
try {
    // Code that may throw exceptions
}
catch (ExceptionType1& e) {
    // Handle ExceptionType1
}
catch (ExceptionType2& e) {
    // Handle ExceptionType2
```

```
}
// ...
```

- Each catch block has a parameter (typically a reference to an exception object) that captures information about the thrown exception. You can access this information to diagnose and handle the error.
- The order of catch blocks matters. The program will execute the first catch block whose exception type matches the thrown exception. Subsequent catch blocks will be skipped.

**The** catch (...) **Catch-All Block**

Sometimes, you may want to handle exceptions of any type in a uniform manner. This is where the catch (...) block comes into play:

```
try {
    // Code that may throw exceptions
}
catch (ExceptionType1& e) {
    // Handle ExceptionType1
}
catch (ExceptionType2& e) {
    // Handle ExceptionType2
}
catch (...) {
    // Handle all other exceptions
}
```

The catch (...) block serves as a catch-all for any unhandled exceptions. It can be useful for logging, cleanup, or providing a generic error message.

**Example: Using** try **and** catch

Let's look at an example of using try and catch to handle a file input error:

```
#include <iostream>
```

```cpp
#include <fstream>
#include <stdexcept>

int main() {
    try {
        std::ifstream
file("nonexistent.txt");
        if (!file.is_open()) {
            throw std::runtime_error("Failed
to open the file.");
        }
        // File operations here
    }
    catch (const std::exception& e) {
        std::cerr << "Exception: " <<
e.what() << std::endl;
    }

    return 0;
}
```

In this code, we attempt to open a file that does not exist. If the file cannot be opened, we throw a std::runtime_error. The catch block then handles this exception and prints an error message.

try and catch blocks provide a structured way to handle exceptions and ensure that your program can gracefully recover from errors, improving its reliability and user experience.

# 9.3 Throwing and Catching Exceptions

Exception handling in C++ involves two essential activities: **throwing** exceptions, which indicate that an exceptional situation has occurred, and **catching** exceptions, which specify how to handle those exceptions.

## Throwing Exceptions

To throw an exception, you use the throw statement within the try block to signal that an exceptional condition has occurred. You can throw exceptions of different types, including built-in types and user-defined types (such as custom exception classes).

*Syntax for Throwing Exceptions*

```
throw ExceptionType("Description of the
exception");
```

- ExceptionType: The type of the exception being thrown. This can be a standard exception type (e.g., std::runtime_error) or a custom exception class.
- "Description of the exception": A human-readable message describing the reason for the exception.

*Example of Throwing an Exception*

```
#include <iostream>
#include <stdexcept>

int divide(int dividend, int divisor) {
    if (divisor == 0) {
        throw std::runtime_error("Division
by zero is not allowed.");
    }
    return dividend / divisor;
}

int main() {
    try {
        int result = divide(10, 0);
        std::cout << "Result: " << result <<
std::endl;
    }
    catch (const std::exception& e) {
```

```
        std::cerr << "Exception: " <<
e.what() << std::endl;
    }

    return 0;
}
```

In this example, the divide function throws a std::runtime_error exception when an attempt is made to divide by zero. The exception is caught and handled in the catch block, which prints an error message.

## Catching Exceptions

Catching exceptions involves using catch blocks to handle exceptions of specific types. Each catch block can handle different types of exceptions and provide appropriate error-handling logic.

*Syntax for Catching Exceptions*

```
try {
    // Code that may throw exceptions
}
catch (ExceptionType1& e) {
    // Handle ExceptionType1
}
catch (ExceptionType2& e) {
    // Handle ExceptionType2
}
// ...
```

- ExceptionType1, ExceptionType2, etc.: The types of exceptions that this catch block can handle.
- e: A parameter (typically a reference) that captures information about the thrown exception. You can access this information to diagnose and handle the error.

*Example of Catching Exceptions*

```cpp
#include <iostream>
#include <stdexcept>

int main() {
    try {
        int result = 10 / 0; // Attempting
division by zero
        std::cout << "Result: " << result <<
std::endl;
    }
    catch (const std::exception& e) {
        std::cerr << "Exception: " <<
e.what() << std::endl;
    }

    return 0;
}
```

In this example, an attempt to divide by zero results in a std::runtime_error exception. The exception is caught and handled in the catch block, which prints an error message.

**Re-Throwing Exceptions**

In some cases, you may want to catch an exception, perform some handling or logging, and then re-throw the same exception or a different one. To re-throw an exception, you use the throw statement within a catch block.

```cpp
try {
    // Code that may throw exceptions
}
catch (ExceptionType1& e) {
    // Handle ExceptionType1
    throw; // Re-throw the same exception
}
catch (ExceptionType2& e) {
```

```
// Handle ExceptionType2
throw AnotherException("Custom error
message");
}
```

Re-throwing exceptions allows you to propagate exceptions up the call stack while still performing specific actions within the catch block.

# 9.4 Custom Exception Classes

While C++ provides a range of built-in exception classes, there are situations where you may need to create custom exception classes tailored to your application's specific requirements. Custom exception classes allow you to provide more detailed and meaningful error information, making it easier to diagnose and handle exceptional conditions in your code.

**Why Use Custom Exception Classes?**

Custom exception classes offer several benefits:

1. **Better Error Reporting:** Custom exceptions can carry additional information, such as error codes, context-specific details, or custom error messages, making it easier to identify and address issues.
2. **Distinct Exception Types:** Custom exceptions allow you to define distinct types of exceptions for different error scenarios within your application. This makes it clearer which errors are being handled.
3. **Hierarchical Exception Structures:** You can create exception hierarchies with base and derived custom exception classes, allowing you to catch exceptions at different levels of granularity.

## Creating a Custom Exception Class

To create a custom exception class, you typically derive it from one of the standard exception classes, such as std::exception or its subclasses like std::runtime_error. You can then add your own members and customize the behavior as needed.

```cpp
#include <iostream>
#include <stdexcept>

class CustomException : public
std::runtime_error {
public:
    CustomException(const std::string&
message) : std::runtime_error(message) {}
};

int main() {
    try {
        // Simulate an error and throw a
custom exception
        throw CustomException("Custom
exception message");
    }
    catch (const CustomException& e) {
        std::cerr << "Custom Exception: " <<
e.what() << std::endl;
    }
    catch (const std::exception& e) {
        std::cerr << "Standard Exception: "
<< e.what() << std::endl;
    }

    return 0;
}
```

In this example, we've created a custom exception class CustomException derived from std::runtime_error. We've provided a

constructor that accepts a custom error message, and the what()
function inherited from std::runtime_error returns this message.

## Using Custom Exception Classes

When an exceptional condition occurs in your code, you can throw
instances of your custom exception class to indicate the error. Catch
blocks can then handle these custom exceptions along with standard
exceptions.

```
try {
    // Code that may throw custom exceptions
}
catch (const CustomException& e) {
    // Handle CustomException
}
catch (const std::exception& e) {
    // Handle other exceptions
}
```

Using custom exception classes enhances the clarity and
maintainability of your code by providing a way to communicate
specific error situations effectively.

## Exception Hierarchies

Custom exception classes can be organized into hierarchies to
represent different categories or levels of errors. This allows you to
catch exceptions at varying levels of detail.

```
class NetworkException : public
std::runtime_error {
public:
    NetworkException(const std::string&
message) : std::runtime_error(message) {}
};

class ConnectionException : public
NetworkException {
```

```cpp
public:
    ConnectionException(const std::string&
message) : NetworkException(message) {}
};

int main() {
    try {
        // Simulate a network error and
throw a specific exception
        throw
ConnectionException("Connection failed.");
    }
    catch (const NetworkException& e) {
        std::cerr << "Network Exception: "
<< e.what() << std::endl;
    }
    catch (const std::exception& e) {
        std::cerr << "Standard Exception: "
<< e.what() << std::endl;
    }

    return 0;
}
```

In this example, we have a hierarchy of network-related exceptions. Throwing a ConnectionException allows us to catch it specifically, while still providing a catch-all for other exceptions.

Custom exception classes are a powerful tool for enhancing the robustness and maintainability of your code. By creating well-structured custom exception hierarchies and providing informative error messages, you can make it easier to handle exceptional conditions and troubleshoot issues in your software.

# 10: FILE HANDLING

## 10.1 Reading and Writing to Files

Reading and writing to files is a fundamental file handling task in C++. It enables your programs to interact with data stored in files on your computer's file system. Whether you're reading configuration settings, processing large datasets, or storing user-generated content, mastering file I/O (Input/Output) is crucial.

### Opening and Closing Files

Before you can read or write data to a file, you need to open it. C++ provides the fstream class, which allows you to create, open, read, and write files. Here's a basic example of opening a file for writing:

```cpp
#include <iostream>
#include <fstream>

int main() {
    // Create an ofstream object (for
writing)
    std::ofstream outputFile("example.txt");

    // Check if the file opened successfully
    if (!outputFile.is_open()) {
        std::cerr << "Error opening file!"
<< std::endl;
        return 1; // Return an error code
    }
```

```cpp
    // Write data to the file
    outputFile << "Hello, File I/O!" <<
std::endl;

    // Close the file when done
    outputFile.close();

    return 0;
}
```

In this example, we:

1. Create an ofstream (output file stream) object named outputFile.
2. Check if the file opened successfully using the is_open() method.
3. Write data to the file using the << operator.
4. Close the file using the close() method.

**Writing to Text Files**

Writing to text files involves treating the file as a sequence of characters. You can use the << operator to insert data into the file, just like you would with the standard output stream (std::cout).

```cpp
#include <iostream>
#include <fstream>

int main() {
    std::ofstream outputFile("example.txt");

    if (!outputFile.is_open()) {
        std::cerr << "Error opening file!"
<< std::endl;
        return 1;
    }

    // Writing to the file
```

```
    outputFile << "Line 1: Hello, File I/O!"
<< std::endl;
    outputFile << "Line 2: Writing to a text
file." << std::endl;

    outputFile.close();

    return 0;
}
```

## Reading from Text Files

Reading from text files involves treating the file as a stream of characters. You can use the >> operator or getline() function to extract data from the file.

```
#include <iostream>
#include <fstream>
#include <string>

int main() {
    std::ifstream inputFile("example.txt");

    if (!inputFile.is_open()) {
        std::cerr << "Error opening file!"
<< std::endl;
        return 1;
    }

    std::string line;

    // Reading lines from the file using
getline
    while (std::getline(inputFile, line)) {
        std::cout << line << std::endl;
    }

    inputFile.close();

    return 0;
```

}

In this example, we:

1.  Create an ifstream (input file stream) object named inputFile.
2.  Check if the file opened successfully.
3.  Use std::getline() to read lines from the file and display them on the console.

Remember to close the file when you're done with it to free up system resources and ensure data integrity.

Reading and writing to files is a core skill in C++ programming. It allows your applications to interact with external data sources and persistently store information. Whether you're working with configuration files, log files, or data files, understanding file I/O is essential for building versatile and data-driven software.

## 10.2 File Streams

File streams in C++ provide a powerful and flexible way to perform file I/O operations. They allow you to read and write data to files using stream-based operations, similar to how you work with the standard input and output streams (std::cin and std::cout).

**Stream-Based File I/O**

C++ provides three main classes for file streams:

*   ifstream: Input file stream, used for reading from files.
*   ofstream: Output file stream, used for writing to files.
*   fstream: File stream, which combines the capabilities of both input and output file streams, allowing you to read from and write to the same file.

These file stream classes are part of the Standard Library's <fstream> header.

## Opening Files with File Streams

To perform file I/O with file streams, you first need to open a file. The open() method is used for this purpose. Here's how to open a file for reading with an ifstream:

```cpp
#include <iostream>
#include <fstream>

int main() {
    std::ifstream inputFile;

    // Open a file for reading
    inputFile.open("example.txt");

    if (!inputFile.is_open()) {
        std::cerr << "Error opening file!" << std::endl;
        return 1;
    }

    // Read data from the file using
inputFile

    inputFile.close();

    return 0;
}
```

Similarly, you can open a file for writing with an ofstream:

```cpp
#include <iostream>
#include <fstream>

int main() {
    std::ofstream outputFile;

    // Open a file for writing
    outputFile.open("output.txt");
```

```cpp
    if (!outputFile.is_open()) {
        std::cerr << "Error opening file!"
<< std::endl;
        return 1;
    }

    // Write data to the file using
outputFile

    outputFile.close();

    return 0;
}
```

**Stream-Based File Operations**

Once you've opened a file, you can use stream operators (<< for output, >> for input) to perform I/O operations. For example, to write data to a file:

```cpp
#include <iostream>
#include <fstream>

int main() {
    std::ofstream outputFile;

    outputFile.open("output.txt");

    if (!outputFile.is_open()) {
        std::cerr << "Error opening file!"
<< std::endl;
        return 1;
    }

    // Write data to the file
    outputFile << "Hello, File Streams!" <<
std::endl;
    outputFile << 42 << std::endl;
```

```
    outputFile.close();

    return 0;
}
```

And to read data from a file:

```cpp
#include <iostream>
#include <fstream>
#include <string>

int main() {
    std::ifstream inputFile;

    inputFile.open("example.txt");

    if (!inputFile.is_open()) {
        std::cerr << "Error opening file!"
<< std::endl;
        return 1;
    }

    std::string line;

    // Read data from the file
    while (std::getline(inputFile, line)) {
        std::cout << line << std::endl;
    }

    inputFile.close();

    return 0;
}
```

**Automatic File Closure**

One of the advantages of using file streams is that they automatically close the file when they go out of scope or when their destructor is called. This means you don't have to explicitly call close() in most cases, improving code readability and reducing the risk of resource leaks.

# 10.3 Error Handling in File Operations

Error handling is a crucial aspect of file operations. Files may not always be available, might have restricted permissions, or may contain unexpected data. Proper error handling ensures that your program can gracefully handle these scenarios and respond appropriately.

**Checking for File Open Errors**

When opening files for reading or writing, it's essential to check if the operation was successful. You can do this by examining the stream's state using the .is_open() member function:

```cpp
#include <iostream>
#include <fstream>

int main() {
    std::ifstream inputFile;

    inputFile.open("nonexistent.txt"); // Try to open a non-existent file

    if (!inputFile.is_open()) {
        std::cerr << "Error opening file!" << std::endl;
        return 1;
    }

    // Read data from the file

    inputFile.close();

    return 0;
}
```

In this example, if the file "nonexistent.txt" doesn't exist or couldn't be opened for any reason, we check the stream's state with !inputFile.is_open() and handle the error accordingly.

## Handling File Reading and Writing Errors

File reading and writing operations may also encounter errors. For instance, you might attempt to read more data from a file than it contains, or you could run out of disk space while writing. To handle these errors, you can check the stream's state after the read or write operation:

```cpp
#include <iostream>
#include <fstream>
#include <string>

int main() {
    std::ofstream outputFile;

    outputFile.open("output.txt");

    if (!outputFile.is_open()) {
        std::cerr << "Error opening file!" << std::endl;
        return 1;
    }

    // Attempt to write to the file
    outputFile << "Hello, File Handling!" << std::endl;

    // Check for write errors
    if (outputFile.fail()) {
        std::cerr << "Error writing to file!" << std::endl;
        return 2;
    }

    outputFile.close();
```

```
        return 0;
}
```

In this example, we first check if the file "output.txt" was successfully opened. Then, after attempting to write data to the file, we check if the stream's state indicates a failure with outputFile.fail(). If an error occurs during the write operation, we handle it accordingly.

## Exception Handling

While checking the stream's state with if statements is a common way to handle file errors, you can also use exception handling to catch and handle exceptions that may be thrown during file operations. C++ file streams can throw exceptions of type std::ios_base::failure for various errors. To enable exception handling for file streams, you can use the exceptions() member function:

```cpp
#include <iostream>
#include <fstream>
#include <string>

int main() {
    std::ofstream outputFile;

    try {
        // Enable exception handling for the
file stream

outputFile.exceptions(std::ofstream::failbit
| std::ofstream::badbit);

        outputFile.open("output.txt");

        // Attempt to write to the file
        outputFile << "Hello, File
Handling!" << std::endl;

        outputFile.close();
```

```
    }
    catch (const std::ios_base::failure& e)
{
        std::cerr << "File operation error:
" << e.what() << std::endl;
        return 1;
    }

    return 0;
}
```

In this example, we use the exceptions() function to specify that the file stream should throw exceptions for both failures (failbit) and severe errors (badbit). When an error occurs, a std::ios_base::failure exception is thrown, which we catch and handle in the try-catch block.

Using exception handling can provide more detailed error information and simplify error propagation in complex programs.

Proper error handling is essential when working with files to ensure the reliability and robustness of your applications. Whether you choose to use if statements to check the stream's state or enable exception handling, it's important to anticipate and gracefully handle errors that may occur during file operations.

# 11: STANDARD TEMPLATE LIBRARY (STL)

## 11.1 Introduction to STL

The Standard Template Library (STL) is a fundamental part of C++ that provides a collection of template classes and functions to simplify complex programming tasks. It is one of the defining features of modern C++ and offers a wide range of reusable components for data manipulation and algorithm implementation. The STL is designed to enhance code reusability, readability, and performance, making it an indispensable tool for C++ developers.

**What Is the STL?**

The STL consists of several components that collectively form a versatile toolkit for C++ programmers:

1. **Containers:** Containers are data structures that store and manage collections of objects. The STL includes a variety of containers like vectors, lists, sets, maps, and more. Each container serves a specific purpose and has unique characteristics, allowing you to choose the most suitable one for your needs.
2. **Algorithms:** Algorithms are a set of functions that operate on containers to perform common tasks such as sorting, searching, and data manipulation. STL algorithms are designed to work with any container that meets certain requirements, offering generic and efficient solutions.
3. **Iterators:** Iterators act as a bridge between containers and algorithms. They allow you to traverse the elements of a

144

container, making it possible to apply algorithms to container data without concern for the underlying data structure.

4. **Function Objects (Functors):** Functors are objects that behave like functions. They are used to customize the behavior of certain algorithms or to encapsulate specific operations. Functors can be easily integrated into STL algorithms.

5. **Utilities:** The STL provides utility classes and functions that simplify common programming tasks. These utilities cover areas such as mathematical operations, type traits, and memory management.

## Advantages of Using the STL

The STL offers numerous advantages to C++ developers:

- **Code Reusability:** STL components are highly reusable. By using them, you can avoid reinventing the wheel and focus on solving the specific problems in your applications.
- **Efficiency:** STL containers and algorithms are designed for high performance. They are often optimized and thoroughly tested, making them a reliable choice for various applications.
- **Standardization:** The STL is a standardized part of the C++ language, which means it's consistent and well-supported across different C++ compilers and platforms.
- **Readability:** STL code tends to be concise and expressive, making it easier to read and maintain.
- **Interoperability:** STL components work seamlessly with each other, allowing you to combine containers, algorithms, and iterators to create powerful solutions.
- **Safety:** Many STL components provide bounds checking and error handling, reducing the risk of common programming mistakes.

## When to Use the STL

The STL is a valuable resource for a wide range of applications, including:

- Data manipulation and processing
- Sorting and searching
- Data structures and algorithms
- Numerical and scientific computing
- Game development
- System-level programming

In essence, the STL is suitable for any scenario where you need efficient and reusable tools to work with data.

## 11.2 Containers (Vectors, Lists, Maps)

STL containers are a fundamental building block of the Standard Template Library. They provide efficient and flexible data storage solutions for a wide range of programming scenarios.

### 11.2.1 Vectors

**Vectors** are dynamic arrays that provide fast and efficient random access to elements. They automatically manage memory and can grow or shrink as needed. Here's how to use vectors:

```cpp
#include <iostream>
#include <vector>

int main() {
    // Create a vector of integers
    std::vector<int> numbers;

    // Add elements to the vector
    numbers.push_back(1);
    numbers.push_back(2);
    numbers.push_back(3);

    // Access elements
    std::cout << "First element: " <<
numbers[0] << std::endl;
```

```cpp
    // Iterate through the vector
    for (const int& num : numbers) {
        std::cout << num << " ";
    }
    std::cout << std::endl;

    // Get the size of the vector
    std::cout << "Vector size: " <<
numbers.size() << std::endl;

    return 0;
}
```

### 11.2.2 Lists

**Lists** are doubly-linked lists that provide fast insertions and deletions at both ends of the container. They are particularly useful when you need to maintain a sorted collection or frequently perform insertions and removals. Here's how to use lists:

```cpp
#include <iostream>
#include <list>

int main() {
    // Create a list of strings
    std::list<std::string> names;

    // Add elements to the list
    names.push_back("Alice");
    names.push_back("Bob");
    names.push_back("Charlie");

    // Insert an element in the middle
    auto it = names.begin();
    ++it; // Move to the second element
    names.insert(it, "David");

    // Iterate through the list
    for (const std::string& name : names) {
        std::cout << name << " ";
```

```
    }
    std::cout << std::endl;

    // Get the size of the list
    std::cout << "List size: " <<
names.size() << std::endl;

    return 0;
}
```

### 11.2.3 Maps

**Maps** are associative containers that store key-value pairs. They allow efficient lookup and retrieval of values based on their keys. Here's how to use maps:

```cpp
#include <iostream>
#include <map>

int main() {
    // Create a map of names and ages
    std::map<std::string, int> ages;

    // Add key-value pairs to the map
    ages["Alice"] = 25;
    ages["Bob"] = 30;
    ages["Charlie"] = 22;

    // Access values by key
    std::cout << "Age of Bob: " <<
ages["Bob"] << std::endl;

    // Check if a key exists
    if (ages.find("David") != ages.end()) {
        std::cout << "Age of David: " <<
ages["David"] << std::endl;
    }
    else {
        std::cout << "David's age not
found." << std::endl;
```

```
    }

    // Iterate through the map
    for (const auto& pair : ages) {
        std::cout << pair.first << ": " <<
pair.second << " years old" << std::endl;
    }

    // Get the size of the map
    std::cout << "Map size: " << ages.size()
<< std::endl;

    return 0;
}
```

These are just a few examples of the STL containers. The STL offers a wide array of containers, each tailored to specific needs, such as sets, queues, and stacks. Choosing the right container for your task can significantly impact the efficiency and maintainability of your code.

## 11.3 Iterators

Iterators are a crucial component of the Standard Template Library (STL) that enable you to traverse and manipulate the elements stored in various STL containers. They provide a uniform way to access container elements regardless of the container's underlying data structure.

### 11.3.1 What Are Iterators?

An **iterator** is an object that acts like a pointer to elements in a container. It provides a way to access and manipulate container elements sequentially. Iterators abstract the details of how the container is organized, allowing you to work with containers in a generic and container-agnostic manner.

## 11.3.2 Types of Iterators

The STL defines several types of iterators, each with specific characteristics and use cases:

1. **Input Iterators:** These iterators allow read-only access to elements and support operations like dereferencing (\*) and incrementing (++). They are suitable for algorithms that only need to read elements from a container once.
2. **Output Iterators:** These iterators allow write-only access to elements and support operations like dereferencing (\*) and incrementing (++). They are used when you need to write data into a container sequentially.
3. **Forward Iterators:** Forward iterators provide read-write access to elements and support dereferencing, incrementing, and equality comparison (==). They are suitable for algorithms that traverse a container in a forward direction.
4. **Bidirectional Iterators:** Bidirectional iterators, in addition to the operations supported by forward iterators, also support decrementing (--). They allow traversal in both forward and backward directions.
5. **Random-Access Iterators:** Random-access iterators provide the most extensive set of operations, including addition (+), subtraction (-), comparison (<, >, <=, >=), and more. They allow efficient random access to container elements, making them suitable for algorithms that require jumping to specific positions within the container.

## 11.3.3 Using Iterators

Let's see how to use iterators with an example using a vector:

```
#include <iostream>
#include <vector>

int main() {
    std::vector<int> numbers = {1, 2, 3, 4,
5};
```

```
    // Using an iterator to traverse the
vector
    std::vector<int>::iterator it;
    for (it = numbers.begin(); it !=
numbers.end(); ++it) {
        std::cout << *it << " ";
    }
    std::cout << std::endl;

    return 0;
}
```

In this example:

- We create a vector called numbers containing integer values.
- We declare an iterator it and initialize it to numbers.begin(), which points to the first element of the vector.
- We use a for loop to iterate through the vector from the beginning (numbers.begin()) to the end (numbers.end()).
- Within the loop, we dereference the iterator (*it) to access the current element.

The use of iterators provides a generic and consistent way to access elements across various STL containers. Whether you're working with vectors, lists, maps, or any other container, iterators allow you to perform common operations like traversal, modification, and searching.

### 11.3.4 Iterator Functions

STL containers also provide member functions that simplify iterator operations. For example, you can use begin() and end() member functions to obtain iterators pointing to the beginning and end of a container, respectively:

```
std::vector<int> numbers = {1, 2, 3, 4, 5};
std::vector<int>::iterator first =
numbers.begin();
```

```
std::vector<int>::iterator last =
numbers.end();
```

Using these member functions enhances code readability and reduces the need for explicit iterator declarations.

### 11.3.5 Algorithms and Iterators

One of the strengths of iterators is their seamless integration with STL algorithms. STL algorithms, such as std::sort, std::find, and std::for_each, are designed to work with iterators, making it easy to apply these algorithms to different containers without modifying your code significantly.

Here's an example of using std::find with iterators to search for an element in a vector:

```cpp
#include <iostream>
#include <vector>
#include <algorithm>

int main() {
    std::vector<int> numbers = {1, 2, 3, 4,
5};
    int target = 3;

    std::vector<int>::iterator it =
std::find(numbers.begin(), numbers.end(),
target);

    if (it != numbers.end()) {
        std::cout << "Element " << target <<
" found at position " <<
std::distance(numbers.begin(), it) <<
std::endl;
    } else {
        std::cout << "Element " << target <<
" not found." << std::endl;
    }
```

```
    return 0;
}
```

In this example, std::find takes two iterators and searches for the specified element in the range defined by those iterators.

# 11.4 Algorithms (Sort, Search, etc.)

The Standard Template Library (STL) provides a rich collection of algorithms that can be used with STL containers. These algorithms cover a wide range of operations, including sorting, searching, data manipulation, and more. In this section, we'll explore some of the most commonly used STL algorithms and how to apply them in your C++ programs.

### 11.4.1 The Power of STL Algorithms

STL algorithms are designed to work seamlessly with STL containers, making them a powerful tool for solving various programming tasks. They offer several advantages:

- **Reusability:** STL algorithms are highly reusable. You can use the same algorithm with different containers, reducing code duplication and enhancing maintainability.
- **Performance:** STL algorithms are typically optimized for efficiency, which can lead to faster and more reliable code.
- **Genericity:** Algorithms are designed to work with a wide range of data types, thanks to C++ templates. This genericity allows you to write flexible and versatile code.

### 11.4.2 Sorting Algorithms

Sorting is a common task in programming, and the STL provides efficient sorting algorithms that work with various container types. The most commonly used sorting algorithm is std::sort. Here's how to use it:

```cpp
#include <iostream>
#include <vector>
#include <algorithm>

int main() {
    std::vector<int> numbers = {5, 2, 9, 1,
5, 6};

    // Sort the vector in ascending order
    std::sort(numbers.begin(),
numbers.end());

    // Print the sorted vector
    for (const int& num : numbers) {
        std::cout << num << " ";
    }
    std::cout << std::endl;

    return 0;
}
```

In this example, we use std::sort to sort the elements in the numbers vector in ascending order. The result is a sorted vector containing {1, 2, 5, 5, 6, 9}.

### 11.4.3 Searching Algorithms

Searching algorithms help you find elements in a container based on specific criteria. The std::find algorithm is commonly used to search for an element in a container. Here's an example:

```cpp
#include <iostream>
#include <vector>
#include <algorithm>

int main() {
    std::vector<int> numbers = {1, 2, 3, 4,
5};
    int target = 3;
```

```
    // Use std::find to search for 'target'
in the vector
    std::vector<int>::iterator it =
std::find(numbers.begin(), numbers.end(),
target);

    if (it != numbers.end()) {
        std::cout << "Element " << target <<
" found at position " <<
std::distance(numbers.begin(), it) <<
std::endl;
    } else {
        std::cout << "Element " << target <<
" not found." << std::endl;
    }

    return 0;
}
```

In this example, std::find is used to search for the element target in the numbers vector. If the element is found, the iterator it points to the found element, and its position is determined using std::distance.

### 11.4.4 Other Common STL Algorithms

The STL provides a plethora of algorithms for various tasks, including:

- **std::for_each:** Applies a function to each element in a range.
- **std::count and std::count_if:** Count the occurrences of an element or elements that satisfy a predicate.
- **std::accumulate:** Computes the sum of elements in a range.
- **std::transform:** Applies a unary or binary operation to elements and stores the results in another container.
- **std::copy and std::copy_if:** Copies elements from one range to another.
- **std::remove and std::remove_if:** Removes elements from a range based on a value or predicate.

- **std::max_element and std::min_element:** Find the maximum and minimum elements in a range.
- **std::reverse:** Reverses the order of elements in a range.

These are just a few examples of the many algorithms available in the STL. Understanding and mastering these algorithms can significantly enhance your C++ programming skills, as they allow you to write efficient and expressive code for a wide range of tasks.

Incorporating STL algorithms into your programs can lead to more readable and maintainable code, as well as improved performance, as many of these algorithms are highly optimized. Whether you're sorting data, searching for elements, or performing other data manipulations, the STL provides a toolbox of reliable and efficient algorithms to simplify your programming tasks.

# 11.5 Custom Data Structures

While the Standard Template Library (STL) provides a wide array of containers and algorithms for common programming tasks, there are situations where you may need to work with custom data structures that are not part of the standard library.

## 11.5.1 Why Custom Data Structures?

There are several reasons why you might need custom data structures in your programs:

- **Domain-Specific Requirements:** Your application may have specific data storage needs that are not met by the standard STL containers. For example, you might need a data structure tailored to represent game entities or financial transactions.
- **Performance Optimization:** In certain scenarios, you may need to optimize data structures for specific operations, such as minimizing memory usage or achieving faster lookup times. Custom data structures allow you to fine-tune performance.

- **Data Encapsulation:** Custom data structures can encapsulate data and behavior into a single unit, providing better data abstraction and maintainability.

## 11.5.2 Creating Custom Data Structures

To create a custom data structure in C++, you typically define a class or struct that encapsulates the data you want to store and any relevant member functions to operate on that data. Here's an example of a simple custom data structure representing a point in 2D space:

```cpp
#include <iostream>

class Point2D {
public:
    Point2D(int x, int y) : x_(x), y_(y) {}

    int getX() const {
        return x_;
    }

    int getY() const {
        return y_;
    }

private:
    int x_;
    int y_;
};

int main() {
    Point2D point(3, 4);
    std::cout << "X coordinate: " <<
point.getX() << std::endl;
    std::cout << "Y coordinate: " <<
point.getY() << std::endl;

    return 0;
```

```
}
```

In this example, we define a Point2D class with two private member variables x_ and y_ to represent the coordinates of a point. The class provides public member functions getX() and getY() to access these coordinates.

### 11.5.3 Integrating Custom Data Structures with STL

You can easily integrate custom data structures with STL containers and algorithms by ensuring that your custom data structures meet the requirements expected by the STL. These requirements include:

- **Copy Constructor:** If your custom data structure needs to be copied, you should define a copy constructor.
- **Assignment Operator (operator=):** Implement the assignment operator if your data structure can be assigned to another object.
- **Comparison Operators (operator==, operator!=, operator<, etc.):** Define comparison operators if you need to compare instances of your custom data structure.
- **Iterator Support:** Implement iterator functionality if you want to use your data structure with STL algorithms. This involves defining functions like begin() and end() that return iterators to the beginning and end of your data structure.
- **Destructor:** If your data structure allocates resources that need to be cleaned up, define a destructor.

Here's an example of how to use a custom data structure with an STL algorithm. Suppose we have a custom Person structure:

```cpp
#include <iostream>
#include <vector>
#include <algorithm>

struct Person {
    std::string name;
    int age;
```

```cpp
    Person(const std::string& n, int a) :
name(n), age(a) {}
};

int main() {
    std::vector<Person> people = {
        {"Alice", 30},
        {"Bob", 25},
        {"Charlie", 35},
        {"David", 28}
    };

    // Sort people by age
    std::sort(people.begin(), people.end(),
[](const Person& a, const Person& b) {
        return a.age < b.age;
    });

    for (const Person& p : people) {
        std::cout << p.name << " (" << p.age
<< " years old)" << std::endl;
    }

    return 0;
}
```

In this example, we define a custom Person struct and sort a vector of Person objects by age using std::sort. We provide a lambda function as the comparison function to customize the sorting behavior.

### 11.5.4 Benefits of Custom Data Structures

Custom data structures offer several benefits:

- **Tailored Functionality:** You can design your data structure to precisely fit your application's requirements, leading to more efficient and intuitive code.

- **Data Encapsulation:** Custom data structures encapsulate data and behavior, promoting better code organization and reusability.
- **Performance Optimization:** You have full control over the data structure's internal representation, allowing for performance optimizations tailored to your specific use case.

However, it's essential to strike a balance between custom data structures and the use of standard STL containers when appropriate. Overusing custom data structures can lead to code complexity and reduced maintainability. It's often wise to leverage the STL's built-in containers and algorithms unless you have a compelling reason to create custom data structures.

Custom data structures are a valuable tool in your programming toolkit, allowing you to address unique programming challenges and optimize your code for specific tasks. When used judiciously, they can enhance the clarity, efficiency, and functionality of your C++ programs.

# 12: BEST PRACTICES AND CODING STYLE

## 12.1 C++ Coding Conventions

Coding conventions are a set of guidelines and rules that developers follow to ensure consistency and readability in their code. Consistent coding conventions make it easier for developers to understand and maintain code, especially when multiple people collaborate on a project. In the world of C++, adhering to coding conventions is an essential part of writing clean, maintainable, and professional code.

### The Importance of Coding Conventions

Coding conventions serve several crucial purposes in C++ development:

1. **Readability:** Consistent naming, formatting, and structure make code more readable. This is especially valuable when you or your team revisit the code weeks, months, or even years after writing it.
2. **Maintainability:** Code that adheres to conventions is easier to maintain. When everyone follows the same style and structure, it's simpler to identify and fix issues, add new features, or make changes.
3. **Collaboration:** When multiple developers work on a project, coding conventions provide a common language and style. This consistency reduces conflicts and misunderstandings among team members.

4. **Debugging:** Clear, well-organized code is easier to debug. It's simpler to locate problems, set breakpoints, and examine variables when the code follows conventions.

## Common C++ Coding Conventions

While coding conventions can vary from project to project and organization to organization, there are some common conventions widely adopted by the C++ community:

### 1. Naming Conventions

- **Use CamelCase for Class Names:** Class names should start with an uppercase letter and use CamelCase (e.g., MyClass, CarModel).
- **Use lowercase for Variable and Function Names:** Variable and function names should start with a lowercase letter and use lowercase with underscores (e.g., my_variable, calculate_total()).
- **Use UPPERCASE for Constants:** Constants should be in all uppercase with underscores (e.g., PI, MAX_VALUE).

### 2. Indentation and Formatting

- **Use Consistent Indentation:** Whether you prefer tabs or spaces, use a consistent indentation style throughout your codebase.
- **Limit Line Length:** Keep lines of code reasonably short (e.g., 80-120 characters) to improve readability.
- **Use Braces for Control Structures:** Always use braces {} to enclose the bodies of control structures (e.g., if, for, while) to avoid ambiguity.

### 3. Comments and Documentation

- **Use Meaningful Comments:** Add comments to explain complex or non-obvious code sections. Comments should be concise and meaningful.

- **Document Function Signatures:** Include comments describing the purpose, input parameters, and return value of functions.
- **Use Doxygen or Similar Tools:** Consider using documentation generators like Doxygen to generate documentation from your code comments.

## 4. Header Files and Include Guards

- **Use Header Guards:** Use include guards (e.g., #pragma once or traditional #ifndef, #define, #endif) to prevent multiple inclusions of the same header file.
- **Include What You Use:** Include only the headers you need in a source file to minimize dependencies and compilation times.

## 5. Naming Conventions for Enums and Constants

- **Use Enum Class:** Prefer using enum classes (scoped enums) over traditional enums to avoid global namespace pollution.
- **Use Prefixes for Constants:** Prefix constants with "k_" (e.g., kPi, kMaxAttempts) to distinguish them from variables.

## 6. Error Handling

- **Use Exceptions for Error Handling:** In C++, exceptions are a preferred mechanism for handling errors and exceptional cases.
- **Return Codes:** If you choose to use error codes, define clear and consistent error code values and document their meanings.

## Adapting to Project-Specific Conventions

While there are common coding conventions, specific projects or organizations may have their own conventions and guidelines. It's crucial to adapt to these conventions when working on such projects.

Clear communication within the team and adhering to the established conventions are essential for successful collaboration.

## 12.2 Debugging Techniques

Debugging is an integral part of the software development process. No matter how experienced you are as a C++ programmer, encountering bugs in your code is inevitable. Debugging is the process of identifying, isolating, and fixing these bugs.

### 12.2.1 Debugging Process

Debugging is not a haphazard activity but a systematic process. Here's an overview of the typical steps involved in debugging C++ code:

1. **Reproduce the Bug:** Start by understanding how to reproduce the bug consistently. Identify the inputs, conditions, or actions that trigger the issue.
2. **Isolate the Problem:** Narrow down the problem's scope. Determine which part of the code is causing the bug. Divide and conquer by isolating the problematic code.
3. **Examine the Code:** Carefully review the relevant code sections. Look for logical errors, incorrect assumptions, or unexpected behavior.
4. **Use Debugging Tools:** Employ debugging tools and techniques to gain insights into the program's state. Common debugging tools include breakpoints, watches, and stack traces.
5. **Print Debugging:** Use print statements (e.g., std::cout or printf) strategically to output information about variables, conditions, or program flow. Print statements can be valuable for understanding what's happening inside your code.
6. **Interactive Debugging:** Most Integrated Development Environments (IDEs) provide interactive debugging tools that allow you to set breakpoints, step through code, inspect variables, and evaluate expressions. Familiarize yourself with your IDE's debugging features.

7. **Analyze Error Messages:** Pay close attention to error messages and warnings generated by the compiler or runtime. They often provide clues about the nature of the problem.

8. **Consult Documentation:** Refer to documentation, including C++ standard libraries and third-party libraries, to ensure you're using functions and classes correctly.

9. **Code Review:** If you're working in a team, seek assistance from colleagues. A fresh pair of eyes can spot issues you may have missed.

10. **Experiment and Test:** Make small, controlled changes to the code to see how they affect the bug. Test different scenarios to understand the bug's behavior better.

11. **Fix and Verify:** Once you've identified the root cause of the bug, implement a fix. Verify that the fix resolves the issue and doesn't introduce new problems.

12. **Regression Testing:** After fixing a bug, conduct regression testing to ensure that other parts of the codebase have not been affected negatively.

## 12.2.2 Common Debugging Tools

Here are some common debugging tools and techniques you can use when debugging C++ code:

*1. Breakpoints:*

- Set breakpoints in your code using your IDE. Execution will pause at these points, allowing you to inspect variables and the program's state.

*2. Watches and Expressions:*

- Use watches to monitor specific variables or expressions during debugging. The debugger will display their values as you step through the code.

*3. Call Stack:*

- Examine the call stack to understand the sequence of function calls leading to the current point in your code. This can help trace the bug's origin.

*4. Profiling Tools:*

- Profiling tools like gprof, Valgrind, or built-in profiling tools in your IDE can help identify performance bottlenecks and memory-related issues.

*5. Memory Debugging:*

- Tools like Valgrind and AddressSanitizer can help detect memory leaks, buffer overflows, and other memory-related issues.

*6. Static Analysis:*

- Use static analysis tools to analyze your code for potential issues before running it. Tools like Clang Static Analyzer and Cppcheck can be valuable.

*7. Logging:*

- Incorporate logging into your code to record program behavior. Log messages can help you trace the execution flow and identify issues.

*8. Assertion Checks:*

- Include assertions (assert in C++) in your code to validate assumptions about the program's state. Assertions can help catch issues early during development.

### 12.2.3 Tips for Effective Debugging

Here are some additional tips to enhance your debugging skills:

- **Be Patient:** Debugging can be a time-consuming process. Approach it with patience and persistence.
- **Keep Records:** Maintain a record of your debugging sessions, including what you've tried, what you've learned, and any solutions you've found. This can be valuable for future reference.
- **Test Incrementally:** When making changes to your code, test one change at a time. This makes it easier to pinpoint the exact cause of the bug.
- **Use Version Control:** If you introduce changes while debugging, consider using version control systems (e.g., Git) to track and manage code revisions.
- **Understand the Domain:** A deep understanding of the problem domain can help you anticipate and identify issues more effectively.
- **Learn from Mistakes:** Debugging is a learning experience. Every bug you encounter is an opportunity to improve your coding skills.

Effective debugging is a skill that improves with practice and experience. It's an essential aspect of writing reliable and robust C++ programs. By following a systematic debugging process, using the right tools, and maintaining a patient and methodical approach, you can become a proficient C++ debugger and tackle even the most challenging bugs in your code.

# 12.3 Performance Optimization

In C++, performance optimization plays a crucial role, especially in applications where speed and resource efficiency are critical. While writing correct and maintainable code is essential, optimizing your code can significantly improve execution speed, reduce memory consumption, and enhance the overall user experience.

### 12.3.1 When to Optimize

Before diving into optimization techniques, it's important to understand when optimization is necessary. Premature optimization, or optimizing code that doesn't need it, can lead to increased complexity and reduced maintainability. Here are some guidelines for when to consider optimization:

1. **Profile First:** Use profiling tools to identify bottlenecks in your code. Profiling reveals where your program spends the most time and helps you focus your optimization efforts on the critical areas.
2. **Performance Requirements:** If your application has specific performance requirements or must meet certain speed or resource constraints, optimization becomes crucial.
3. **Data-Intensive Operations:** Operations involving large datasets, such as data processing, image manipulation, or scientific computing, often benefit from optimization.
4. **Real-Time Systems:** Applications that operate in real-time, such as video games or control systems, must be highly optimized to meet tight deadlines.

### 12.3.2 Optimization Strategies

When optimizing C++ code, consider the following strategies:

*1. Algorithm Selection:*

- Choose the most appropriate algorithms and data structures for your problem. A more efficient algorithm can provide substantial performance gains.

*2. Data Locality:*

- Optimize data access patterns to improve cache locality. Accessing data that is closer in memory can be significantly faster than accessing scattered memory locations.

*3. Avoid Unnecessary Work:*

- Eliminate redundant computations, unnecessary memory allocations, and repetitive operations. Cache results and reuse them when possible.

*4. Inline Small Functions:*

- Mark small, frequently called functions as inline to reduce the function call overhead.

*5. Compiler Optimization:*

- Enable compiler optimizations (-O2, -O3, etc.) to let the compiler generate more efficient machine code. Modern C++ compilers are highly capable of optimizing code.

*6. Multithreading and Parallelism:*

- Utilize multithreading and parallelism to leverage multiple CPU cores for concurrent execution when applicable. Libraries like the C++ Standard Library's <thread> and <future> can assist with this.

*7. Memory Management:*

- Be mindful of memory allocation and deallocation. Minimize dynamic memory allocations and use object pooling or custom memory management techniques when necessary.

*8. Profiling and Benchmarking:*

- Regularly profile and benchmark your code to measure performance improvements accurately. Tools like gprof, perf, and third-party profilers can provide valuable insights.

*9. Compiler Directives:*

- Explore compiler-specific directives and pragmas to guide optimizations (e.g., GCC's __attribute__ or Visual C++'s #pragma optimize).

*10. Platform-Specific Optimization:*

- Tailor optimizations to the target platform. Different architectures may benefit from specific optimizations.

### 12.3.3 Common Performance Pitfalls

Avoid common performance pitfalls that can hinder optimization efforts:

1. **Premature Optimization:** As mentioned earlier, don't optimize code prematurely. Profile first to identify the performance bottlenecks.
2. **Micro-Optimizations:** Focus on high-impact optimizations rather than micro-optimizations that have minimal impact on overall performance.
3. **Ignoring Compiler Warnings:** Compiler warnings can highlight potential performance issues. Address them to ensure the best optimization results.
4. **Ignoring Caching Effects:** Understanding memory hierarchies and caching can help you optimize data access patterns effectively.
5. **Ignoring Multithreading:** In multi-core systems, leveraging parallelism can provide significant performance improvements. Don't overlook this opportunity.
6. **Neglecting Testing:** After optimizing, thoroughly test your code to ensure correctness and stability. Optimization changes can introduce new bugs.

### 12.3.4 Measuring Performance

Measuring performance is essential to ensure that your optimization efforts are effective. Use benchmarking tools and profilers to assess the impact of your optimizations. Monitor metrics like execution time, memory usage, and CPU utilization. Be cautious of measurement overhead when interpreting results.

### 12.3.5 Optimizing with Care

While performance optimization is important, it should not compromise code readability, maintainability, or correctness. Striking a balance between optimization and maintainability is crucial. Document your optimizations, explain the reasoning behind them, and consider the trade-offs involved.

Remember that optimization should be based on evidence and data from profiling, rather than assumptions. Continuously monitor and profile your code to detect performance regressions and address them promptly.

# 13: FINAL PROJECTS AND REAL-WORLD APPLICATIONS

## 13.1 Building a Simple Application

In this first project of the final chapter, you'll create a simple C++ application from scratch. This project is designed to help you practice and apply the core concepts you've learned throughout this book. While the application itself may be straightforward, the process of building it is a valuable learning experience.

### 13.1.1 Project Overview

**Project Goal:** Create a command-line application that performs a useful task or solves a specific problem. The exact functionality of your application is open to your creativity and interests.

**Key Objectives:**

1. **Design:** Plan and design your application. Consider its purpose, user interface (even if it's a command line), and data handling.
2. **Implementation:** Write the C++ code to implement your application's functionality.
3. **Testing:** Test your application thoroughly to ensure it works correctly and handles different scenarios gracefully.
4. **Documentation:** Provide clear documentation that explains how to use your application, including any command-line arguments or user instructions.

## 13.1.2 Project Ideas

Here are a few project ideas to consider, though you are encouraged to come up with your own based on your interests and goals:

1. **Task Manager:** Build a simple command-line task manager that allows users to add, list, and remove tasks.
2. **Calculator:** Create a command-line calculator that performs basic arithmetic operations.
3. **Text File Analyzer:** Develop a tool that analyzes text files, counting words, lines, or specific patterns.
4. **To-Do List:** Build a to-do list application that lets users manage their tasks, set priorities, and mark items as completed.
5. **Number Converter:** Create a utility that converts between different number bases (e.g., decimal to binary).
6. **File Renamer:** Build a program that renames files in a directory based on user-defined rules.

## 13.1.3 Project Workflow

Here's a general workflow to guide you through this project:

**1. Project Planning:**

- Define the purpose and functionality of your application.
- Plan the structure of your code, including classes, functions, and data structures.
- Decide on any external libraries or dependencies you may need.

**2. Implementation:**

- Write the C++ code for your application, following best practices and coding conventions.
- Handle user input and any command-line arguments.
- Implement the core functionality of your application.

**3. Testing:**

- Test your application thoroughly. Try different input scenarios to ensure it behaves as expected.
- Debug and fix any issues you encounter during testing.
- Consider writing unit tests if applicable.

## 4. Documentation:

- Write clear and concise documentation for your application. Include instructions on how to use it.
- Provide examples and sample commands to help users get started.

## 5. Refinement:

- Review your code for potential improvements and optimizations.
- Consider user feedback and make necessary enhancements.

## 6. Finalization:

- Ensure your code is well-organized, well-documented, and follows coding standards.
- Create a release version of your application, ready for distribution.

### 13.1.4 Learning and Growth

Building a simple C++ application is a rewarding experience that allows you to apply your knowledge in a practical context. Throughout this project, you'll encounter challenges and problem-solving opportunities, which are essential for your growth as a programmer.

As you work on your application, remember that the skills and principles you've learned in this book—such as good code structure, debugging techniques, and coding conventions—will serve as your foundation. This project is not just about the end result but also about the process of learning, creating, and improving.

So, choose a project idea that excites you, roll up your sleeves, and start building your C++ application. The journey begins here, and the possibilities are endless!

# 13.2 Intermediate and Advanced Projects

While building a simple C++ application is a great way to apply your foundational skills, intermediate and advanced projects take your programming journey to the next level. These projects challenge you to explore more complex concepts, tackle larger problems, and gain hands-on experience with advanced C++ features.

### 13.2.1 Why Choose Intermediate and Advanced Projects?

Intermediate and advanced projects offer several benefits:

1. **Deepen Your Knowledge:** These projects require a deeper understanding of C++ concepts, algorithms, and data structures.
2. **Problem Solving:** You'll encounter more challenging problems and have the opportunity to develop creative solutions.
3. **Enhanced Skills:** Complex projects often involve working with libraries, frameworks, or APIs, which can expand your skill set.
4. **Real-World Applications:** These projects often mirror real-world scenarios, providing valuable experience for your career or personal projects.

### 13.2.2 Project Ideas

Here are some project ideas that fall into the intermediate and advanced categories:

*Intermediate Projects:*

1. **Text-Based Game:** Develop an interactive text-based game with multiple levels, choices, and storytelling elements.

2. **Database Application:** Create a C++ application that interacts with a SQLite or MySQL database to perform CRUD (Create, Read, Update, Delete) operations.
3. **Multi-threaded Application:** Build a multi-threaded program that demonstrates parallel processing, such as a file downloader or image processing tool.
4. **Networking Chat Application:** Design a client-server chat application using sockets and network programming concepts.
5. **Simulation Software:** Develop simulation software that models real-world scenarios, such as traffic simulations, weather modeling, or population dynamics.

*Advanced Projects:*

1. **3D Graphics Engine:** Create a 3D graphics engine that renders 3D models, handles shaders, and supports user interaction.
2. **Compiler or Interpreter:** Develop a simple programming language compiler or interpreter, complete with lexical analysis, parsing, and code generation.
3. **Machine Learning Application:** Implement a machine learning algorithm (e.g., neural networks, decision trees) from scratch or use a library like TensorFlow in a C++ project.
4. **Embedded Systems Project:** Build a project for an embedded system or microcontroller, such as a home automation system or IoT device.
5. **High-Performance Computing:** Work on a project that harnesses the power of high-performance computing clusters or GPUs for scientific simulations or data analysis.

### 13.2.3 Project Development Process

Developing intermediate and advanced projects requires careful planning and a systematic approach:

1. **Project Definition:** Clearly define the project's goals, requirements, and scope. Consider what you want to achieve and any constraints you'll face.

2.  **Research and Design:** Spend time researching the technologies, libraries, and tools you'll need. Create a detailed design or architecture for your project.
3.  **Implementation:** Write well-structured, maintainable code while following best practices. Break your project into manageable modules or components.
4.  **Testing and Debugging:** Rigorously test your project at each stage of development. Use debugging tools and techniques to identify and resolve issues.
5.  **Optimization:** Optimize your code for performance, memory usage, and scalability. Profiling tools can help you identify bottlenecks.
6.  **Documentation:** Provide thorough documentation, including user guides and developer documentation. Make it easy for others (or yourself) to understand and use your project.
7.  **Version Control:** Use version control systems like Git to track changes and collaborate with others if applicable.
8.  **Deployment:** Prepare your project for deployment. This may involve packaging, installation scripts, or setting up a server.

### 13.2.4 Continuous Learning

Intermediate and advanced projects are not only about the end result but also about the learning journey. Embrace the challenges, be prepared to overcome obstacles, and stay open to exploring new technologies and concepts. These projects are an opportunity to push your boundaries and become a more proficient C++ developer.

Remember that building complex projects can take time, patience, and persistence. Be prepared to iterate, refine, and learn from your experiences. Whether it's for personal growth or career advancement, these projects will leave a lasting impact on your programming journey.

# 13.3 C++ in Industry and Open Source Projects

### 13.3.1 C++ in Industry

C++ plays a significant role in a wide range of industries and domains:

*1. Game Development:*

- Many video games, especially high-performance and graphics-intensive ones, are developed using C++ for its speed and control over hardware resources.

*2. System Programming:*

- Operating systems like Linux and Windows are partially or entirely written in C++ due to its low-level capabilities.

*3. Finance and Trading:*

- In the finance sector, C++ is popular for developing trading platforms, algorithmic trading systems, and quantitative analysis tools.

*4. Aerospace and Aviation:*

- C++ is used in avionics software, flight simulators, and control systems for its real-time capabilities and reliability.

*5. Automotive Industry:*

- Automotive manufacturers use C++ for in-car entertainment systems, engine control units, and autonomous vehicle software.

*6. Telecommunications:*

- Networking equipment, communication protocols, and telecom software are often written in C++.

*7. Healthcare and Medical Devices:*

- C++ is utilized in medical imaging, robotic surgery systems, and diagnostic equipment.

*8. Graphics and Multimedia:*

- Graphics engines, image and video processing software, and digital audio workstations rely on C++ for performance.

*9. Scientific Computing:*

- Numerical simulations, computational chemistry, and physics simulations are written in C++ to take advantage of its computational speed.

*10. Embedded Systems:*

- C++ is employed in embedded systems for industries like IoT, home automation, and industrial automation.

C++ is chosen for these industries because of its ability to deliver high-performance code, fine-grained memory control, and extensive libraries and frameworks.

### 13.3.2 C++ in Open Source Projects

C++ is a prominent language in the open source community, contributing to a wide array of projects and libraries. Here's why C++ is a favored choice in this ecosystem:

*1. Performance-Critical Projects:*

- Open source projects that require high performance, such as game engines (e.g., Unreal Engine), multimedia libraries (e.g., FFmpeg), and scientific computing tools (e.g., ROOT), often rely on C++.

*2. Cross-Platform Development:*

- C++ is suitable for cross-platform development, making it easier to create open source software that works on various operating systems.

*3. Compatibility with C Libraries:*

- C++ can easily interface with C libraries, enabling open source projects to leverage existing C codebases and libraries.

*4. Resource Management:*

- C++ provides powerful resource management capabilities, allowing open source projects to efficiently manage memory, files, and other resources.

*5. Strong Type Safety:*

- C++'s strong type system aids in writing robust and reliable open source software.

*6. Community Collaboration:*

- C++ has an active and dedicated open source community, which contributes to the development and maintenance of libraries and tools.

*7. Stability and Longevity:*

- Many open source projects built in C++ have stood the test of time, offering stable and well-maintained solutions to a variety of problems.

### 13.3.3 Contributing to Open Source Projects

If you're interested in getting involved in open source C++ projects, consider the following steps:

1. **Choose a Project:** Find an open source project that aligns with your interests and skills. Platforms like GitHub and GitLab are great places to discover and contribute to projects.
2. **Study the Codebase:** Familiarize yourself with the project's codebase, documentation, and development guidelines.
3. **Start Small:** Begin with small contributions, such as bug fixes, documentation improvements, or adding tests.
4. **Collaborate and Communicate:** Engage with the project's community through mailing lists, forums, or chat channels. Effective communication is key to successful collaboration.
5. **Follow Best Practices:** Adhere to coding standards, version control practices, and testing conventions established by the project.
6. **Learn and Grow:** Contributing to open source projects is a valuable learning experience. It allows you to work with experienced developers, understand real-world codebases, and enhance your skills.

Whether you're contributing to open source or working in an industry-specific domain, C++ offers a powerful and versatile platform for software development. It continues to be a language of choice for those who seek both performance and control in their projects.

# APPENDIX

## Commonly Used Library Functions

The C++ Standard Library provides a rich set of functions and classes to simplify common programming tasks, from input/output operations to data manipulation and algorithmic operations.

**1.** Input/Output (I/O) Functions:

- **cin and cout:** Standard input and output streams for reading from and writing to the console.
- **getline():** Reads a line of text from an input stream, often used for reading strings.
- **printf() and scanf():** Functions for formatted input and output, commonly used in C-style I/O.

**2.** String Functions:

- **strlen():** Returns the length (number of characters) of a C-style string.
- **strcpy() and strncpy():** Copy one string to another.
- **strcmp():** Compare two strings lexically.
- **strcat():** Concatenate (append) one string to another.
- **strstr():** Find the first occurrence of a substring in a string.
- **strtok():** Tokenize a string based on a delimiter.

**3.** Container Functions:

- **std::vector:** A versatile dynamic array with methods like push_back(), pop_back(), and size().

- **std::map and std::unordered_map:** Associative containers for key-value pairs.
- **std::set and std::unordered_set:** Containers for storing unique values.
- **std::deque:** Double-ended queue for efficient insertion and deletion at both ends.

**4.** Algorithm Functions:

- **std::sort():** Sorts elements in a container (e.g., array, vector) in ascending order.
- **std::reverse():** Reverses the order of elements in a container.
- **std::find():** Searches for a value in a container and returns an iterator.
- **std::count():** Counts the occurrences of a value in a container.
- **std::max() and std::min():** Returns the maximum and minimum values among a set of values.

**5.** Math Functions:

- **std::abs():** Computes the absolute value of an integer or floating-point number.
- **std::sqrt():** Calculates the square root of a number.
- **std::pow():** Raises a number to a specified power.
- **std::ceil() and std::floor():** Round a floating-point number up or down.
- **std::rand():** Generates a random integer within a specified range.

**6.** File I/O Functions:

- **std::ifstream and std::ofstream:** Stream classes for reading and writing files.
- **std::getline():** Reads a line from a file.
- **std::feof() and std::ferror():** Check for end-of-file and file error conditions.

**7.** Memory Management Functions:

- **new and delete operators:** Allocate and deallocate dynamic memory.
- **malloc() and free():** C-style memory allocation and deallocation.
- **std::unique_ptr and std::shared_ptr:** Smart pointers for automatic memory management.

**8.** Time and Date Functions:

- **std::chrono:** Provides utilities for measuring time intervals and durations.
- **std::time():** Returns the current system time.
- **std::ctime():** Converts a time value to a human-readable string.

These are just a selection of commonly used library functions and features available in the C++ Standard Library. Familiarizing yourself with these functions can greatly accelerate your development process and help you write efficient, maintainable code. As you become more proficient in C++, you'll discover many more functions and classes that cater to various programming tasks.

# Key C++ Terminology

C++ is a powerful and versatile programming language with its own set of terminology and concepts. Understanding these terms is essential for becoming proficient in C++. Here are some key C++ terminology and concepts you should know:

**1.** Variable:

A variable is a named storage location in memory that holds data. Variables can have different types, such as integers, floating-point numbers, characters, and custom user-defined types. In C++, you declare variables with a specific type to indicate the kind of data they can hold.

## 2. Data Type:

A data type specifies the kind of data that a variable can hold. Common data types in C++ include int (integer), double (floating-point number), char (character), and bool (Boolean). C++ allows you to define custom data types through structures and classes.

## 3. Function:

A function is a reusable block of code that performs a specific task. Functions are defined with a name, a parameter list (if any), a return type (if any), and a body that contains the code to execute. C++ programs often consist of multiple functions, including the main() function, which serves as the entry point.

## 4. Class:

A class is a blueprint for creating objects. It defines the structure and behavior of objects by specifying attributes (data members) and methods (member functions). Objects created from a class are instances of that class and can interact with each other.

## 5. Object:

An object is an instance of a class. It is a concrete representation of the class's blueprint, with its own set of data members and methods. Objects are used to model real-world entities and encapsulate their behavior and data.

## 6. Method:

A method, also known as a member function, is a function defined within a class. Methods define the behavior of objects created from the class. They can manipulate the object's data and perform operations specific to that class.

## 7. Constructor:

A constructor is a special member function in a class that gets called when an object of the class is created. Constructors initialize the object's data members and set up its initial state. C++ allows multiple constructors with different parameter lists.

## 8. Destructor:

A destructor is a special member function in a class that gets called when an object is destroyed or goes out of scope. Destructors are used to clean up resources allocated by the object, such as memory or file handles.

## 9. Inheritance:

Inheritance is a fundamental concept in object-oriented programming. It allows a class (the derived class or subclass) to inherit the properties and methods of another class (the base class or superclass). This promotes code reuse and the creation of hierarchical class structures.

## 10. Polymorphism:

Polymorphism allows objects of different classes to be treated as objects of a common base class. It enables dynamic method dispatch, allowing you to call methods on objects without knowing their specific derived types. C++ achieves polymorphism through virtual functions and function overriding.

## 11. Encapsulation:

Encapsulation is the practice of bundling data (attributes) and methods (functions) that operate on that data into a single unit, known as a class. It enforces data hiding and abstraction, allowing the internal details of a class to remain hidden from external code.

## 12. Abstraction:

Abstraction is the process of simplifying complex systems by breaking them down into smaller, more manageable parts. In C++, classes and objects provide a way to abstract real-world entities and their behavior.

## 13. Namespace:

A namespace is a container for organizing identifiers (variables, functions, classes, etc.) to prevent naming conflicts. It helps manage the scope and visibility of symbols in a C++ program. The standard library components are often organized in the std namespace.

## 14. Template:

Templates in C++ allow you to write generic code that can work with different data types. Function templates and class templates enable you to create flexible and reusable code components.

## 15. STL (Standard Template Library):

The Standard Template Library is a collection of template classes and functions that provide common data structures (e.g., vectors, lists, maps) and algorithms (e.g., sorting, searching) for C++ programmers. It simplifies data manipulation and algorithm implementation.

## 16. Header File:

A header file (usually with a .h extension) contains declarations for functions, classes, and constants that can be used in multiple source files. Header files are included in source files using #include directives.

**17.** Source File:

A source file (usually with a .cpp extension) contains the actual implementation of functions and classes declared in header files. Source files are compiled to produce executable programs.

**18.** Compiler:

A compiler is a software tool that translates human-readable C++ code into machine-readable binary code (object code) that can be executed by a computer. Popular C++ compilers include GCC, Clang, and Microsoft Visual C++.

These key C++ terminology and concepts provide a foundation for understanding the language's fundamentals. As you dive deeper into C++ programming, you'll encounter additional concepts and techniques that expand on these fundamental building blocks.